NAVAL

USS Kidd (DD-661)

From WWII and Korea to Museum Ship

DAVID DOYLE

4880 Lower Valley Road Atglen, PA 19310

Library of Congress Control Number: 2022932048

Cover design by Justin Watkinson
Type set in Impact/Minion Pro/Univers LT Std

ISBN: 978-0-7643-6465-5
Printed in China

Published by Schiffer Publishing, Ltd.
4880 Lower Valley Road
Atglen, PA 19310
Phone: (610) 593-1777; Fax: (610) 593-2002
Email: Info@schifferbooks.com
Web: www.schifferbooks.com

Acknowledgments

While working on this book I was blessed with the generous help of Tom Kailbourn, Rick Davis, Tracy White, Bob Steinbrunn, Al Ross, and A. D. Baker, without which the book would have been much more challenging to create. Enormous help, particularly by providing access, came from Tim NesSmith with USS *Kidd*. As always, my wonderful wife, Denise, took notes, scanned photographs, and accompanied me while photographing USS *Kidd*.

Contents

Introduction

The keel of the Fletcher-class destroyer USS *Kidd* was laid at Federal Shipbuilding and Drydock Company in Kearny, New Jersey, on October 18, 1942. In keeping with the US Navy tradition of naming destroyers after naval heroes, this, the 661st destroyer built for the US Navy, was named after RAdm. Isaac Campbell Kidd Sr. As commander of Battleship Division 1 and chief of staff and aide, commander, Battleship Battle Force, Adm. Kidd was aboard his flagship, USS *Arizona* (BB-39), the morning of December 7, 1941. Adm. Kidd's Medal of Honor citation reads, in part, that he "courageously discharged his duties as senior officer present Afloat until *Arizona* blew up from a magazine explosion and a direct bomb hit on the bridge which resulted in the loss of his life."

The destroyer USS *Kidd* was one of four destroyers, along with USS *Bullard* (DD-660), USS *Thorn* (DD-647), and USS *Turner* (DD-648), that were launched on February 28, 1943, in a record-breaking fourteen minutes.

She was sponsored by Mrs. Inez Kidd, widow of RAdm. Kidd, who not only christened her but also presented her crew with a wardroom guest book in which she inscribed, "May the destiny of the USS *Kidd* be glorious! May her victories be triumphant and conclusive!"

The US Navy commissioned 175 Fletcher-class destroyers during World War II, making them the most numerous type of destroyers of the Navy. This is USS *Fletcher*, DD-445, the lead ship of the class, which was designed in 1939 and launched in 1942. *Fletcher* was scrapped in 1972.

USS *Kidd* proudly carries on the tradition of the destroyers that served in the US fleet in World War II, and honors the name of her namesake, RAdm. Isaac C. Kidd, who was killed on the bridge of USS *Arizona* during the December 7, 1941, attack on Pearl Harbor.

CHAPTER 1

World War II

Her first voyage, which was under the command of Cmdr. Allan Roby, was short, merely a move across the harbor from the Federal Shipyard to the Brooklyn Navy Yard. A unique aspect of this voyage was the result of one member of her crew—Ens. Randle. Ens. Randle was Anne Randle, a member of the WAVES (Women Accepted for Voluntary Emergency Service), and was the first member of that service to be assigned to the office of shipbuilding in New York City. She had been ordered to take a training tour of the Kearny facility, and to accompany the destroyer back across the harbor to the Navy Yard. Because of prevalent superstition at the time that having a woman aboard a Navy ship was a bad omen, the ship's roster listed her only as "Ensign A. Randle."

Another unusual aspect of the journey was that *Kidd* flew the "Jolly Roger" from its foremost. Not surprisingly, the crew had adopted the pirate Captain Kidd as their mascot. Being sensitive both to Adm. Kidd's legacy and his widow's feelings, they contacted Mrs. Kidd. From her they learned that the admiral's nickname at the Naval Academy had been "Cap" (as in "Captain Kidd"), and the moniker had stuck with him until his death. Mrs. Kidd even approached the Navy on behalf of the crew, requesting permission to fly the "Jolly Roger" and have an image of the buccaneer painted on the vessel.

With permission granted, the crew collected $400 from among themselves and commissioned a sign painter to paint the pirate on the ship's stack.

After fitting out at the Navy Yard, USS *Kidd* was commissioned April 23, 1943, with Cmdr. Allan Roby as her first commanding officer.

Following her shakedown cruise in Casco Bay, Maine, in June, *Kidd* cruised in the Atlantic near Argentia, Newfoundland, and then served as escort for new carriers on the Caribbean shakedown cruise from Norfolk to Trinidad.

Kidd departed for the Pacific in August 1943, in company with USS *Alabama* (BB-60) and USS *South Dakota* (BB-57), transiting the Panama Canal with the two battleships and three other destroyers.

At 0609 on September 12, 1943, as part of a planned training exercise, *Kidd* simulated an attack on Task Group 34.9 while en route to Pearl Harbor. At 0624 *Kidd* was struck by two 5-inch star shells fired by USS *North Carolina* (BB-55). One shell struck the starboard side at frame 40, penetrating the hull at the waterline and passing through the ship, passing out the port side at the waterline. The other round ricocheted, entering officer's country at frame 63. The casualty of that second hit was *Kidd*'s authorized stock of medical brandy, which had been stored in the safe of the medical officer. Almost as serious, in the forward part of the ship, *Kidd*'s damage control party had been conducting a drill. As part of the drill, Seaman W. A. Jordan had been strapped into a stretcher, as if he were a casualty. The shell passing through the compartment crossed just above Jordan's chest, causing him a minor abrasion. Cmdr. Roby reported to the task group commander that "*Kidd* claims to be the best prepared ship in the Navy. We had a victim already strapped in the stretcher when he was wounded."

Kidd, along with the rest of the task group, arrived at Pearl Harbor on September 17, 1943, and the destroyer tied at the Navy Yard for repairs and replenishment.

Kidd was assigned to escort aircraft carriers toward Wake Island for the heavy air attacks of October 5 and returned to Pearl Harbor on October 11, 1943.

Assigned to Destroyer Division 96 (DesDiv 96) within Destroyer Squadron 48 (DesRon 48), USS *Kidd* was one of many escort ships, along with carriers *Essex* (CV-9), *Bunker Hill* (CV-17), and *Independence* (CV-22), comprising Task Group 50.3 to a strike position south of Rabaul on the morning of November 11, 1943.

A series of photos was taken of the destroyer *Kidd* on April 22, 1943, during delivery to the Navy on the day before she was commissioned. On the bow is the destroyer's number, 661. A 20 mm gun is visible on the low bridge to the front of the square-type pilothouse. As built, two more 20 mm guns were in tubs on the superstructure deck, below the 20 mm mount to the front of the pilothouse; the starboard 20 mm mount on the superstructure deck is visible here. Atop the pilothouse is the Mk. 37 director, at this stage with no radar antenna atop it. The radar installations were not yet present on the foremast. As built, *Kidd* had two 36-inch searchlights on platforms on the sides of the smokestack.

As the carrier aircraft pounded Japanese positions on Rabaul and Bougainville, at 1347 *Kidd* was ordered to pick up the crew of an *Essex* aircraft that had crashed during takeoff. Dropping behind the formation, *Kidd* maneuvered to pick up the three downed airmen.

Now 8 miles astern of the task group, *Kidd* was alone and in the line of flight of twenty Japanese dive-bombers looking to strike back at the Americans pummeling their airfields. The lone destroyer drew the attention of the Japanese, and as the destroyer struggled to avoid airborne torpedoes and bombs, her crew picked up the three airmen, one of whom, ARM3c Ray Bright, was dead. By the time the gunfight was over at 1430 (ten minutes after rescuing the air crew), *Kidd* expended 173 rounds of 5"/38-caliber rounds from her dual-purpose main battery, as well as 1,000 rounds of 40 mm ammunition and 2,100 rounds of 20 mm ammunition. *Kidd*'s gunners brought down three enemy planes, with one more kill probable and hits scored on several of the remaining aircraft. Cmdr. Allan B. Roby was recognized for his part in this action by receiving the Silver Star for gallantry.

About this time, *Kidd* began a tradition befitting her mascot and earning her the nickname "Pirate of the Pacific." Upon returning the pilots to the carriers, *Kidd* would "demand ransom" from the much larger vessels, to be paid in the form of treats not usually found on the much smaller destroyer, such as ice cream.

On the afternoon of November 20, 1943, *Kidd* was a screening unit of Task Group 50.3 when a flight of fifteen Japanese "Betty" torpedo planes passed by en route to attack the troopships at Tarawa. *Kidd* was 15,000 yards away from the task group investigating a reported submarine sighting when the flight of enemy aircraft was spotted. *Kidd* radioed a warning to the task group, then turned broadside to the flight to bring all guns to bear. When the range closed to 7,000 yards, *Kidd* opened fire with her 5-inch mounts, and as the range continued to close, the 40 mm battery joined in. Despite firing 127 rounds of 5-inch and 108 rounds of 40 mm in a well-placed barrage, *Kidd* was able to down only two of the attacking airplanes, which got within 1.5 miles. The Japanese succeeded in scoring one hit on USS *Independence*.

Early December found *Kidd* screening Task Group 50.1 as the force moved against Wotje, Kwajalein, and Maloejap. Most of the time *Kidd* was employed providing antiaircraft fire as well as picking up downed US airmen. On December 4, a Japanese plane was able to get through the screen and place a torpedo in USS *Lexington* (CV-16), knocking out her steering control. *Kidd* was among the group of ships detailed to escort *Lexington* to Pearl Harbor for repair, arriving December 9, 1943. After spending just over a week in training off Hawaii, on December 20, 1943, *Kidd* entered the Navy Yard at Pearl Harbor for repairs to her guns and on Christmas Eve moved to marine railway #2 for scraping and painting her bottom. She went back in the water on December 28.

On January 2, 1944, *Kidd* left Pearl Harbor, escorting the Liberty ship SS *James. B. Francis* to Espiritu Santo via Funafuti. The duo arrived at Funafuti on January 10, and after *Kidd* discharged her passengers, mail, and light freight, the pair steamed onward beginning January 11, arriving at Espiritu Santo on January 15.

The next day, *Kidd* steamed again for Funafuti, escorting USS *William Ward Burrows* (AP-6), arriving January 19. Three days later, she, along with DesDiv 96, left the harbor to rendezvous with a number of troopships and escorts for a landing on Majuro. Preceded only by the minesweepers, *Kidd* entered the atoll there at 0725 on January 31. Reconnaissance troops reported no Japanese on the island, and the planned bombardment was canceled.

On February 3, *Kidd* steamed from Majuro lagoon to join other vessels in blockading Wotje and Taroa lagoons, as well as shelling enemy aircraft facilities on those islands. This operation continued until February 11, when the task group withdrew to Majuro for refueling, arriving the next day. After a one-day respite, the task group returned to Wotje and resumed its operations there, continuing the bombardment until February 18, when once again it withdrew to Majuro. Upon arrival there, *Kidd* was assigned for three days of repair and maintenance by the destroyer tender USS *Prairie* (AD-15).

Repairs complete, *Kidd*, along with USS *Black* (DD-666), escorted USS *Chester* to Kwajalein, arriving there on February 26. On March 4, *Kidd*, along with other destroyers, left Kwajalein and returned to Majuro, arriving the next day. After additional maintenance, on March 10 *Kidd*, along with DesDiv 96 and additional vessels, left for Espiritu Santo. The ships, designated Task Unit 15.16, reached their destination at 1400 on March 15, where they joined Task Force 36. *Kidd* was assigned to Task Group 36.2. On March 23, *Kidd*, along with the rest of DesDiv 96, departed Espiritu Santo to rendezvous with Task Force 58, arriving at Purvis Bay on March 26. April 1 found *Kidd* operating as part of Task Unit 36.3.1, screening the escort carriers *Corregidor* and *Coral Sea*, which had been assigned to provide air coverage at Emirau Island while an airfield was being built there.

On April 16, *Kidd* and numerous other vessels left Purvis Bay bound for the Manus Island area to support the occupation of Aitape Island. By May 1, these operations had expanded to include providing support for the taking of enemy airfields on Hollandia. On May 4, *Kidd* and Task Group 78.1 retired to Manus Island, where she remained until May 7, when she and Task Group 78.4 steamed for Espiritu Santo. After arrival at that anchorage on May 12, *Kidd* underwent maintenance and repair until May 21.

June 14 found *Kidd* as part of Task Group 52.11 assisting in the taking of Saipan. During these operations *Kidd*'s men rescued a downed naval aviator. On June 25, *Kidd* and Task Group 53.1 departed the Saipan area, steaming for Eniwetok, reaching their destination on June 28.

On July 8, *Kidd* was part of a formidable naval force attacking Guam. While a part of the bombardment force, on July 13 *Kidd* narrowly escaped being struck by a Japanese aircraft. These operations continued until *Kidd* and the rest of Task Unit 53.15.11 departed Guam on August 10, during which time *Kidd* was credited with having rescued a total of thirty-five carrier personnel. The task unit reached Eniwetok on August 15, and two days later *Kidd* was part of Task Unit 57.5.10, bound for Pearl Harbor and some much-needed repair and shore leave. She separated from the convoy on August 25 to proceed independently to Pearl Harbor in order to deliver an emergency appendectomy case to the hospital, tying up at the pier B-11, Pearl Harbor, at 0800 on August 26.

From September 3 through 13, *Kidd* was in drydock at Pearl Harbor for repair and modification. Also, on August 29 her beloved captain, Cmdr. Allan Roby, was reassigned and replaced with Cmdr. Harry G. Moore.

October 20 found *Kidd* back in action off Leyte Island, Philippines, supporting the invasion providing fire support as well as antiaircraft protection until October 22, when *Kidd* and Task Unit 79.14.2 withdrew to Hollandia, arriving on October 27. She steamed from Hollandia on November 1, bound for Morotai, where she dropped anchor on November 5. There, from November 5 to 9, the Japanese made nightly raids on the Morotai airfield, but the attacking aircraft were out of range of *Kidd*'s guns.

Kidd steamed from Morotai on November 10, becoming part of landing-force Task Unit 79.15.6, steaming toward Leyte Gulf. On the evening of November 13, a Japanese "Jill" aircraft launched a torpedo at USS *Catskill* (LSV-1), which missed and continued toward *Kidd*. Radical maneuvering allowed *Kidd* to avoid the torpedo. The force reached the landing beaches at dawn on November 14. Two days later, *Kidd* and five other vessels were detached and steamed to Humboldt Bay, New Guinea, arriving at dawn on November 19. *Kidd* remained at anchor there until December 5, when she steamed for Manus Island, anchoring there the next day. On December 9, she departed Seeadler Harbor bound for Pearl Harbor, arriving on December 19 at 0830. After offloading some munitions, she departed at 1400 bound for San Francisco, steaming at 18 knots.

Kidd and her crew anchored in San Francisco Bay on Christmas Eve. On Christmas Day they tied up at Mare Island and offloaded ammunition. The following day she moved into Mare Island Navy Yard for forty-seven days of overhaul and modification, with her crew enjoying, in alternating groups, some much-needed leave.

On February 5, 1945, *Kidd*, repairs largely complete, was moved to the ammunition dock at Navy Ammunition Depot, Mare Island, and took aboard ammunition. After two days of trials, she returned

A starboard-side view of *Kidd* on April 22, 1943, shows the locations of the two 21-inch quintuple-tube torpedo launchers, to the front and the rear of the forward smokestack. On top of the rear launchers is a drum-shaped blast shield, to protect the operators of that mount. The structure between the numbers 3 and 4 5-inch/38-caliber gun mounts contained a fan room, a gun-crew shelter, and ammunition storage; a splinter shield and platform were above that shelter, where a twin 40 mm gun mount soon would be installed.

The aft port quarter of *Kidd* is the focus of this photo, taken on the day before the destroyer's commissioning. Flying from the port yardarm was a "Jolly Roger" pirate flag. The pirate theme was a tradition the ship would continue, on the basis not of the namesake of the ship, RAdm. Isaac Kidd, but on the destroyer's mascot, the pirate William Kidd. On the side of the hull near the stern is the port propeller guard. A similar one was on the starboard side.

to the Navy Yard for final repairs, which were completed on February 9. The next day she put to sea, and her crew began refresher training. On February 19, she steamed for Pearl Harbor, arriving on February 25.

Kidd, as part of Task Group 12.2, got underway for Ulithi, Caroline Islands, on March 3, dropping anchor there on March 13. At that time *Kidd* was assigned to Task Group 59.7 as a screening vessel for the battle line, which included Battleship Divisions Six, Seven, and Eight, and Cruiser Division Sixteen (USS *Guam* and *Alaska*). On March 15, Task Force 59 was dissolved and its units assimilated into famed Task Force 58. The task force struck Kyushu and Honshu at dawn on March 17. On March 19, the carrier *Franklin* was hit by a kamikaze and was badly damaged. *Kidd* was among the vessels providing screening as the cruiser USS *Pittsburgh* took the crippled carrier in tow. On March 22, *Kidd* rejoined Task Group 58.3, which set course for Okinawa. The task group reached a position 75 miles southeast of Okinawa on March 23 and began to launch airstrikes. The next day, shore bombardment of the island began by the fast battleships. Airstrikes and bombardment continued until March 27, when *Kidd* and the balance of DesRon 62, along with CruDiv 17, moved toward Kyushu.

For the remainder of March and into April, *Kidd* continued to operate with Allied forces near the Japanese home islands. On Wednesday, April 11, 1945, 90 miles east of Okinawa, at 1346 hours *Kidd* went to general quarters. Eleven minutes later, *Kidd*'s gunners, as well as those of USS *Bullard* (DD-660), shot down a Japanese airplane attacking *Bullard*. At 1409 a single plane came in low over the water, apparently again targeting *Bullard*. The aircraft passed over Bullard and bore on toward *Kidd*. *Kidd*'s starboard-side 20 mm and 40 mm batteries targeted the enemy, scoring hits but not dissuading it. *Kidd* attempted to take evasive action, but at 1410 the aircraft crashed into the starboard side of the ship, its bomb penetrating the forward fireroom, passing through the ship and rupturing number 1 boiler before exploding just outside the port beam. Thirty-six men were killed aboard *Kidd*, including everyone in the fireroom, two men were missing, and fifty-five, including the captain, the executive officer, and the ship's doctor, Broox C. Garrett Jr., were wounded. The wounded executive officer, Lt. B. H. Brittin, took command at 1411.

At 1639, USS *Hale* (DD-642) came alongside to transfer her doctor aboard using high line. While this effort was being undertaken, *Hale* came under attack by a Japanese bomber. Both *Hale* and *Kidd* opened fire, and the enemy bomb fell 50 yards astern of *Hale* as the enemy retired. The next afternoon, *Kidd*, now escorted by *McNair* (DD-679), joined Task Unit 50.18.7, and *Kidd*'s seriously wounded men, including Cmdr. Moore, transferred to larger, better-equipped ships for treatment.

Kidd, with only one boiler room operational and chief engineer Lt. (jg) George P. Grieshaber among those killed in the attack, and Task Unit 50.18.7 made way for Ulithi Atoll. By splitting the steam between the two engine rooms, *Kidd* was able to make 20 knots. En route, a burial detail was formed, and the dead were committed to the sea on April 12. Lt. Brittin, suffering from his wounds, was unable to remain in command, and on the morning of April 13, Lt. R. L. Kenney assumed temporary command, with Lt. (jg) J. Mathews Jr. as acting executive officer. Pumping continued on the

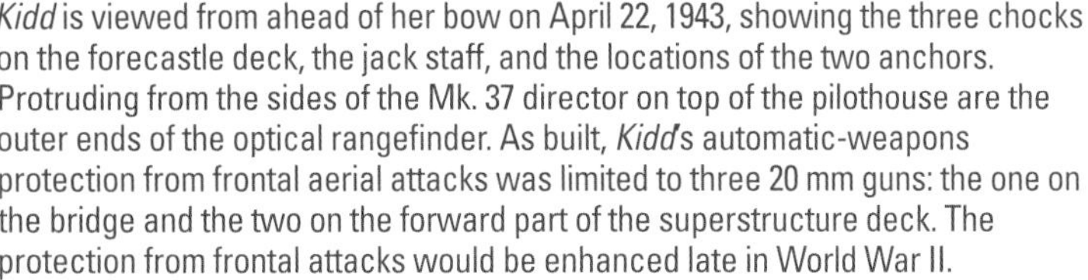

Kidd is viewed from ahead of her bow on April 22, 1943, showing the three chocks on the forecastle deck, the jack staff, and the locations of the two anchors. Protruding from the sides of the Mk. 37 director on top of the pilothouse are the outer ends of the optical rangefinder. As built, *Kidd*'s automatic-weapons protection from frontal aerial attacks was limited to three 20 mm guns: the one on the bridge and the two on the forward part of the superstructure deck. The protection from frontal attacks would be enhanced late in World War II.

In a final April 22, 1943, photograph, on the stern is embossed "KIDD" in raised letters. Above the ship's name are the stern chock and a stanchion holding the stern, anchor, and wake lights. To each side of the stern are racks for four smoke generators and release tracks for depth charges. Under canvas covers and barrels pointed upward, to the rear of the aft 5-inch/38-caliber gun mount are three 20 mm guns.

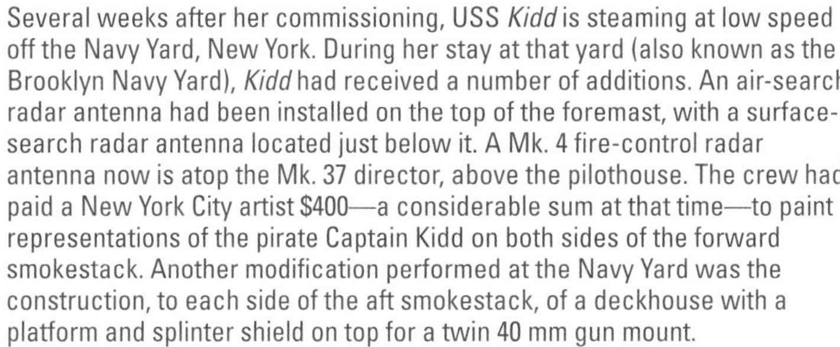
Several weeks after her commissioning, USS *Kidd* is steaming at low speed off the Navy Yard, New York. During her stay at that yard (also known as the Brooklyn Navy Yard), *Kidd* had received a number of additions. An air-search radar antenna had been installed on the top of the foremast, with a surface-search radar antenna located just below it. A Mk. 4 fire-control radar antenna now is atop the Mk. 37 director, above the pilothouse. The crew had paid a New York City artist $400—a considerable sum at that time—to paint representations of the pirate Captain Kidd on both sides of the forward smokestack. Another modification performed at the Navy Yard was the construction, to each side of the aft smokestack, of a deckhouse with a platform and splinter shield on top for a twin 40 mm gun mount.

USS *Kidd* is observed from the port side off the Navy Yard, New York, on May 8, 1943. Initially, the ship was painted in Measure 21 camouflage, with Navy Blue (5-N) on all vertical surfaces and Deck Blue (20-B) on horizontal surfaces. Running along the main deck from abeam the forward torpedo launchers, forward to below the motor whaleboat, is a bulwark; the top of its forward end curved upward. Each of the two new deckhouses with the twin 40 mm gun mounts on top, to the sides of the aft smokestack, contained ready-service ammunition for those guns, as well as a 40 mm control and radar room.

heavily damaged destroyer throughout the trip. Additionally, ammunition in the forward magazines had to be jettisoned to preserve stability.

When *Kidd* reached Ulithi, she tied up alongside the destroyer tender *Hamul* (AD-20) for temporary repairs. In addition to preparing *Kidd* for the long voyage home, the men of *Hamul* cast a brass plaque listing the names of the thirty-eight men killed in the attack. The plaque was mounted on the quarterdeck of the destroyer, where it remains today.

On April 30, Cmdr. Fred M. Bush assumed duties as commanding officer of *Kidd*. Two days later, Bush received orders to get underway for Pearl Harbor. Steaming with two other ships, the battered destroyer reached Pearl Harbor on May 15. After transferring some munitions, the next day *Kidd* stood out for San Francisco. At 0923 *Kidd* tied up at the Ammunition Depot Dock, Mare Island, to offload all ammunition aboard. The offload complete, at 1423 *Kidd* tied up at Berth 8, United States Naval Dry Docks, Hunters Point, to begin permanent repairs to her battle damage. At 1700 on May 31, she entered drydock #6 at Hunters Point, where she would remain until August 1. Postrepair shakedown, refresher training, and final repairs were completed, and the ship steamed for Pearl Harbor on August 20.

The pirate on the stack, which had been ordered painted over in late 1944, was ordered returned by Cmdr. Bush, causing morale among the crew to soar. *Kidd* steamed up the entrance channel to Pearl Harbor on August 26, eleven days after Emperor Hirohito announced his intention to surrender.

The war over, on September 18 *Kidd* steamed from Pearl Harbor back to California, with, in addition to her crew, one hundred enlisted men and fourteen officers as passengers. She arrived at San Diego on September 24 and reported to ComEleven for placing in inactive status in the reserve fleet. On September 26, all explosives and munitions were offloaded. *Kidd*'s crew began the meticulous process of placing the ship in "in commission, in reserve" status, a process that would not be completed until December. After spending a year "in commission, in reserve," on December 10, 1946, USS *Kidd* was finally decommissioned and floated "in mothballs" as a member of the Pacific Reserve Fleet.

As seen in a final photo from May 8, 1943, during the April–May 1943 refitting at the Navy Yard, the 36-inch searchlights had been moved from the sides of the aft smokestack to new platforms on the sides of the forward smokestack. The former searchlight platforms on the aft smokestack now were furnished with splinter shields and held directors for the new amidships twin 40 mm gun mounts. The director for the aft twin 40 mm gun mount is the object with the cover over it on the forward end of the platform for that gun mount. The director was a device that allowed its operator to visually track targets as well as control and fire the associated gun mount. The 40 mm and 5-inch gun mounts also could be fired by their own crews, under what was known as "local control."

This and the next four photos of USS *Kidd* were taken in dock at the Navy Yard, New York, on May 6, 1944. In the foreground is the gallery of three 20 mm guns aft of 5-inch/38-caliber gun mount number 5. All three guns are at maximum elevation; canvas covers are over the two outboard mounts. The handwheel on the pedestal of the center mount was for raising or lowering the gun and cradle. The faces of 5-inch mounts numbers 4 and 5 are in the background. The enclosures for these mounts were not called turrets, but shields. The ports on the frontal shields were for the trainer and the pointer, who, respectively, traversed and elevated the guns during local control.

A view from the starboard side of 5-inch/38-caliber gun mount number 3 (*lower left*) facing forward, shows the recently added twin 40 mm gun mount, splinter shield, platform, and foundation (*right*). Between the 5-inch gun mount and the aft smokestack are the aft quintuple-tube torpedo launchers, and the drum-shaped blast shield for the torpedo operators. A round hatch door at the top of the blast shield is open. Visible above the splinter shields of the platforms on the sides of the aft smokestack are the Mk. 51 directors for the amidships twin 40 mm gun mounts.

Facing astern, in the foreground is the number 4 5-inch/38-caliber gun mount, with details of the buckler, also called blast bag, which sealed the spaces between the gun tube and the shield. Below is the number 5 5-inch gun mount, to the immediate rear of which is the gallery of three 20 mm antiaircraft guns. On the fantail are depth-charge release tracks and smoke generators, and, *at the center*, two recently installed depth-charge storage racks.

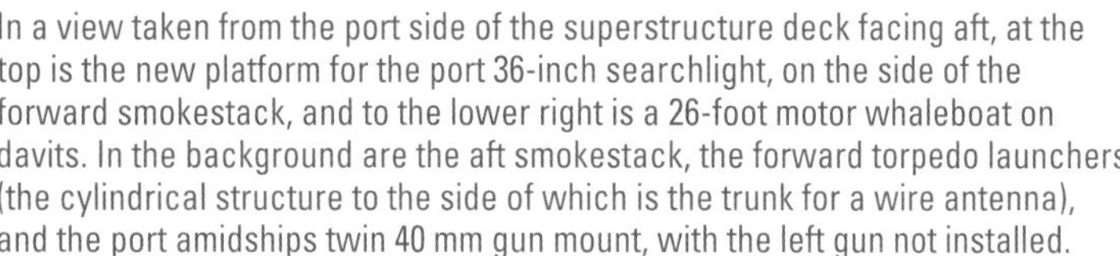

In a view taken from the port side of the superstructure deck facing aft, at the top is the new platform for the port 36-inch searchlight, on the side of the forward smokestack, and to the lower right is a 26-foot motor whaleboat on davits. In the background are the aft smokestack, the forward torpedo launchers (the cylindrical structure to the side of which is the trunk for a wire antenna), and the port amidships twin 40 mm gun mount, with the left gun not installed.

This final photo taken at the Navy Yard, New York, on May 6, 1943, was taken from the top of the pilothouse looking toward the bow. In the foreground is the 20 mm gun mount to the front of the pilothouse, including front and rear gun deflectors, which prevented the gunner from shooting up the upper works of the destroyer in the heat of combat. The destroyer's number, "661," is painted atop the number 2 5-inch/38-caliber gun mount. On the right rear corner of the roof of that mount is the mount captain's hatch. The stanchion on the same roof is for an anchor light.

In a photo taken at sea from another ship in late 1943, probably during an underway replenishment procedure, crewmen of USS *Kidd* are relaxing around the forward smokestack. The original "Captain Kidd" artwork is clearly visible on the stack. Also in view are the foremast at the far left, the steam whistle and the siren on the top front of the smokestack, the port 36-inch searchlight and its platform, a floater-net bin below the "Captain Kidd" artwork, and the forward torpedo crane and torpedo launchers, to the rear of the stack.

Probably on the same occasion as in the preceding photo, crewmen of *Kidd* are standing by on the port Mk. 51 director platform on the aft smokestack. The tube-shaped feature jutting at an angle from below the forward part of the platform is a wire-antenna trunk. Below, on the superstructure deck, are the forward (*left*) and aft quintuple torpedo launchers. The forward launchers were the Mk. 14, and the aft ones, equipped with a blast shield for the crew, were the Mk. 15. The blast shield was necessary for the safety of the crew because of the proximity of the number 3 5-inch/38-caliber gun mount.

A view of *Kidd* from starboard shows damage incurred off Okinawa on April 11, 1945, when a Japanese kamikaze aircraft struck the ship on that side, causing extensive damage and killing or wounding ninety-three crewmen. The ship was repaired at San Francisco. *USS* Kidd *collection*

USS *Kidd* is proceeding at speed in choppy seas. According to the original USN label for the photo, the photo was taken from USS *Colorado* on November 12, 1943. However, *Colorado's* war diary indicates that that battleship was anchored in the harbor at Efate, New Hebrides, on that date and the several days preceding and after that date. An aircraft is visible low above *Kidd's* aft smokestack, and what appear to be antiaircraft artillery bursts are visible to the right of the aircraft carrier in the left background. Thus, there is a chance that this photo was taken on November 11, 1943, when *Kidd* and nearby ships were attacked by several Japanese aircraft. In the attack, *Kidd* claimed three kills.

In an undated photo taken sometime before early January 1945, a photographer aboard the cruiser USS *Honolulu* (CL-48) took this view of USS *Kidd* approaching to deliver mail. The Measure 21 camouflage seen in the April and May 1943 photos had been painted over with a new scheme in May 1944. The new scheme was Measure 32/10D, the "Measure" referring to the specific paint colors employed, and "10D" referring to the design.

Elements of Task Force 52, including USS *Kidd* in the foreground, are preparing to depart from the anchorage at Roi, in Kwajalein Atoll, Marshall Islands, en route to the invasion of Saipan, on June 10, 1944. Anchored to the left is USS *Tennessee* (BB-43), with a difficult-to-discern Fletcher-class destroyer alongside the aft part of the battleship. A light carrier is on the far side of the battleship.

USS *Kidd* underwent modernizations at the Navy Yard, Mare Island, California, from December 26, 1944, to February 10, 1945. She is seen here in the channel off Mare Island on February 8, having just returned from San Francisco Bay, where she underwent speed runs, calibration of compasses and radars, and test-firing of the 5-inch/38-caliber guns. Previously, the ship had been repainted in Measure 22 camouflage, with Navy Blue (5-N) from the boot topping (the black band around the waterline) to the lowest point of the main deck, and Haze Gray (5-H) on all vertical surfaces above that point; the decks and all horizontal surfaces were painted Deck Blue (20-B.) The paint exhibits considerable chipping and weathering.

In a February 8, 1945, photo of USS *Kidd* off Mare Island, a noticeable change is the Mk. 12/22 fire-control radar antenna combination above the Mk. 37 director. This antenna set included a Mk. 12 antenna, for acquiring and tracking targets, and the Mk. 22 antenna, for determining the altitude of the target.

USS *Kidd* is viewed from the port side off Mare Island on February 8, 1945. The three 20 mm gun mounts to the front and below the pilothouse had been removed, and now two twin 40 mm gun mounts were on platforms with splinter shields below and to the front of the bridge, between the front of the superstructure and the rear of 5-inch/38-caliber gun mount number 2.

The Mk. 12/22 fire-control and height-finding antennas are prominent above the Mk. 37 director in a starboard-aft photo of USS *Kidd* on February 8, 1945. The parabolic Mk. 22 antenna was called an "orange-peel antenna" owing to its resemblance to the peel of a segment of an orange.

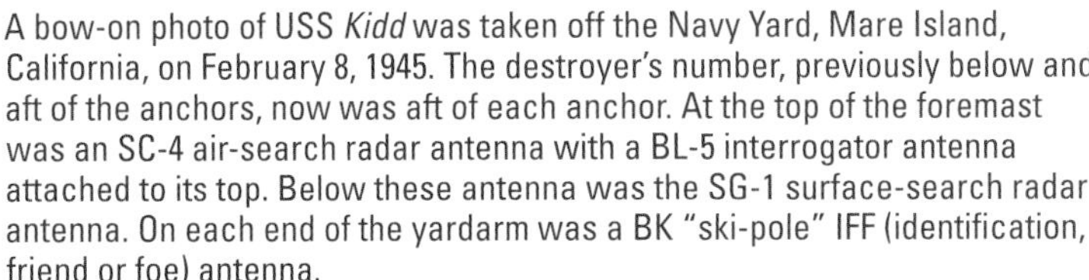

A bow-on photo of USS *Kidd* was taken off the Navy Yard, Mare Island, California, on February 8, 1945. The destroyer's number, previously below and aft of the anchors, now was aft of each anchor. At the top of the foremast was an SC-4 air-search radar antenna with a BL-5 interrogator antenna attached to its top. Below these antenna was the SG-1 surface-search radar antenna. On each end of the yardarm was a BK "ski-pole" IFF (identification, friend or foe) antenna.

On the same date, *Kidd* was photographed from astern. The two racks for smoke generators have been removed. To the starboard side of the port depth-charge release track is a ventilator.

USS *Kidd* is seen from the forward-port quarter at the Navy Yard, Mare Island, on February 8, 1945, with an unidentified, round-bridge, Fletcher-class destroyer to her starboard side. The new twin 40 mm gun mount, platform, and splinter shield below the port side of the bridge are visible. A similar 40 mm mount now was on the opposite side too.

In another dockside view of *Kidd* at Mare Island, bins for floater nets have been installed to the lower rear of the searchlight platform on the forward smokestack and on the splinter shield for the Mk. 51 director on the aft smokestack. Bins also were on the corresponding positions on the starboard side. Floater nets were designed to float free of their bins should the ship be sunk, giving survivors something to keep them afloat until rescued.

During the December 1944 to February 1945 modernizations at Mare Island, alterations were made to the depth-charge release tracks on the fantail and to the stern lights, located on a stanchion above the stern chock. On the main deck to the far left are depth-charge storage racks, interspersed with which were three Mk. 6 depth-charge projectors and loading davits.

During a Japanese aerial attack off Okinawa at 1410 on April 11, 1945, an aircraft, seen here, made it through a barrage of antiaircraft fire from all the destroyer's starboard 20 mm and 40 mm guns, crashing into the starboard side of the ship and passing entirely through the forward fireroom. A bomb carried under the plane exploded off the port side of the hull. Casualties to *Kidd* were thirty-six killed, two missing, and fifty-five, including the captain and the executive officer, wounded. On the following day, *Kidd* departed from the area for Ulithi Atoll for repairs.

A view of *Kidd* from starboard shows damage incurred off Okinawa on April 11, 1945, when a Japanese kamikaze aircraft struck the ship on that side, causing extensive damage and killing or wounding ninety-three crewmen. The ship was repaired at San Francisco. *USS Kidd collection*

USS *Kidd* was at the US Naval Drydocks, Hunters Point, California, from May 31 to August 8, 1945, for a major overhaul, repairs, and modernization. She was photographed off Hunters Point on August 8, the date of her departure for San Diego, California. The destroyer retained her Measure 22 camouflage scheme.

As seen in a portside view of *Kidd* on August 8, 1945, a significant modernization implemented during the May-to-August overhaul at Hunters Point was the installation of quadruple 40 mm antiaircraft gun mounts on the platforms adjacent to the aft smokestack. Each of these mounts was equipped with a radar dish antenna, which fed data on the target range and range rate to the Mk. 51 directors. These radar antennas and directors were part of the newly installed Mk. 63 Gunfire Control System (GFCS). The directors for the quadruple amidships 40 mm gun mounts were installed on the platform atop a new structure between the smokestacks. Installing this structure necessitated removing the forward torpedo launchers.

The DBM-1 and TDY-1 antennas on the new mainmast are in view in this photograph of USS *Kidd* from astern on August 8, 1945. The davits holding the motor whaleboat on the starboard side have been swung out.

USS *Kidd* is viewed bow-on in San Francisco Bay on August 8, 1945. Jutting out slightly from the upper part of both wings of the bridge, but not on the center part of the structure, are wind deflectors, which forced the wind upward, to protect crewmen on the bridge.

Another new feature from the Hunters Point modernizations in 1945 was a mainmast, visible above the aft twin 40 mm gun mount. On the upper part of the mast are two DBM-1 radar direction-finder antennas, below which is a TDY-1 jammer antenna.

Two crewmen on a scaffold plank are touching up the paint on the hull of *Kidd* at Hunters Point on August 7, 1945. Recent modernizations on the ship are circled. On the front of the superstructure, between the first and second 5-inch/38-caliber gun mounts, is a floater-net bin. Below the bridge is the forward-starboard twin 40 mm gun mount, platform, and splinter shield, installed earlier.

In a starboard side view of *Kidd* on August 7, 1945, to the left is the new structure for two Mk. 51 directors, on the superstructure deck. Newly installed antennas are circled. Visible above the bulwark of the bridge are, *left to right*, a searchlight, the starboard torpedo director, a signal searchlight, a pelorus (the bulbous housing on a pedestal), and a Mk. 51 director for the forward starboard twin 40 mm gun mount. The Captain Kidd artwork on the forward smokestack, painted over by the time the ship was overhauled at Mare Island in February 1945, had been repainted.

At Hunters Point in the summer of 1945, the structures for the amidships twin 40 mm gun mounts were revamped, with curved splinter shields on the forward faces; this feature is circled at the center. Between those mounts and the forward smokestack is the new deckhouse and platform for the directors for the amidships 40 mm guns. Circled to the left is the new mast with two DBM-1 radar direction-finder antennas and a TDY-1 jammer antenna. Below that mast is a new rack for two life rafts. Two new twin 20 mm antiaircraft gun mounts are circled on the main deck.

CHAPTER 2

Korean and Cold Wars

When Communist North Korea invaded South Korea on June 25, 1950, the United States and the United Nations rushed to defend the southern country. *Kidd*, which had been only steamed to Pearl Harbor and back to California after overhaul and before being placed in reserve, was in excellent material condition. Not surprisingly, she was one of the ships reactivated to bolster the fleet and stem the Communist aggression.

Kidd was recommissioned March 28, 1951, with Lt. Cmdr. Robert E. Jeffery in command. Following yard work, and after shakedown and training, *Kidd* departed for Yokosuka, Japan, on June 18, 1951, and arrived at that port on July 15. Once there, she was assigned to DesDiv 152 and joined Carrier Task Force 77 at Wonsan, Korea. On October 21, *Kidd* relieved USS *Brown* (DD-546), bombarding targets of opportunity on the eastern coastline of Korea from Nan-Do Island southward below Kansong until January 22, 1952. The next day, *Kidd* and the rest of DesDiv 152 escorted USS *Badoeng Strait* (CVE-116) to Yokosuka Japan Naval Yard, then the destroyers steamed for San Diego.

Entering the Navy Yard at Mare Island, *Kidd* underwent overhaul and modification, during which the forward 40 mm guns were replaced with Hedgehog projectors, newer radar equipment was installed, and the 20 mm guns were removed. Cmdr. C. A. Bellis relieved Cmdr. Jeffery on February 28. 1952,

The yard work was completed on May 17, and after shakedown and refresher training, as well as brief service as a gunnery school ship, on September 8, 1952, *Kidd* and the rest of the division steamed to rejoin Task Force 77 in Korean waters.

In October, *Kidd* took part in the mock invasion near Kojo, Korea, a feint to confuse the enemy. The following month, *Kidd* returned to bombardment duty, as well as resuming one of her World War II activities—picking up downed allied airmen.

On December 10, 1952, near Wonsan, an enemy shore battery fired on *Kidd*. *Kidd*'s 5-inch guns returned fire, silencing the enemy weapons.

On March 3, 1953, *Kidd* steamed once again for her annual overhaul at San Diego, stopping at Midway and Pearl Harbor en route. She arrived in San Diego on March 20. On April 15, 1953, Cmdr. Bellis was relieved by Cmdr. L. B. Ensey.

With her overhaul complete, *Kidd* steamed toward Long Beach on April 20, 1953. The next day, when off Pierpoint Landing in Long Beach Harbor, *Kidd* was rammed by the 9,000-ton Swedish freighter *Hainan*. Fortunately, there were no injuries, but *Kidd* had to enter drydock at Long Beach Naval Shipyard to repair the gaping 15-foot V-shaped hole in the hull that was just forward of the forward 5-inch mount. The gash, which extended 3 feet below the waterline, opened the sonar compartment to the sea, as well as exposing the CPOs' quarters. Repairs were effected, and *Kidd* left the shipyard on May 11, 1953.

Returning to the western Pacific, *Kidd* steamed first to Pearl Harbor, then again to Yokosuka, and rejoined Task Force 77. After a month of steaming with the carriers, *Kidd* put into Sasebo for repair and shore leave. Leaving Japan, she steamed to Hong Kong (China) before steaming through heavy seas on patrol. Following the signing of the Armistice, she continued patrolling waters off Korea and Japan until returning to San Diego for overhaul on May 23, 1954. After completion of that overhaul, *Kidd* alternated Westpac cruises with operations on the West Coast, making stops at Pearl Harbor, Midway, Yokosuka and Sasebo (Japan), Okinawa, Hong Kong (China), New Guinea, and New Zealand.

In September 1957, *Kidd* and her crew got a taste of Hollywood as she and the submarine USS *Redfish* (SS-395) participated in the filming of the motion picture *Run Silent, Run Deep* off the

Deactivated after World War II and placed in long-term storage, USS *Kidd* was recommissioned for service in the Korean War on March 28, 1951. The destroyer is seen around the time she was recommissioned, displaying Measure 13 camouflage: Haze Gray (5-H) on all surfaces except for the decks, which were painted Deck Blue (20-B). The destroyer essentially had the same external appearance and equipment as at the end of World War II.

coast of San Diego, with *Kidd* somewhat ironically portraying a World War II Japanese destroyer.

She visited Sydney, Australia, on March 29, 1958, and later that year patrolled again following the Chinese bombardment of the offshore islands of Quemoy and Matsu.

On January 5, 1960, the "Pirate of the Pacific" left the West Coast, steaming east, the result of her being transferred to the Atlantic Fleet. After transiting the Panama Canal, she arrived in Philadelphia on January 25.

Upon her arrival, her typical duty was making Naval Reserve training cruises to various East Coast and Caribbean ports. That changed on October 2, 1961, when in response to the Soviet construction of the Berlin Wall, *Kidd* joined the fleet operating forces as part of the rapid mobilization of the military. In December of that year, *Kidd* was dispatched to waters off the Dominican Republic in a "show-of-force" patrol to provide an element of security in the troubled Caribbean following the overthrow of the Trujillo dictatorship.

Kidd arrived at Norfolk on February 5, 1962, and joined Task Force Alpha for ASW exercises. Then, on April 24, she was assigned to the Naval Destroyer School at Newport, Rhode Island. After a cruise to the Caribbean, on July 1, 1962, she resumed Naval Reserve training.

Kidd was decommissioned for the final time on June 19, 1964, and was placed "in mothballs" as a unit of the Atlantic Reserve Fleet in Philadelphia. During her twenty years of service, she had earned twelve battle stars during her career: eight for service in World War II and four for service in Korea.

Damage to the upper part of the starboard side of the shell and the main deck is documented in this photo. To the upper left is the shield of 5-inch/38-caliber gun mount number 1. Toward the upper right is a hatch. Repairs to this damage were concluded on May 11, 1953.

From March 20 to April 20, 1953, USS *Kidd* underwent an overhaul at San Diego, California. Following that time in the yard, the destroyer steamed to Long Beach, California, where, on April 21, she was struck by the Swedish freighter *Hainan*, causing considerable damage to the hull and main deck between frames 21 and 30. As seen in this photo, the starboard of the shell (the steel plating on the outside of the hull) was ripped open from the waterline to the main deck. Surveying the damage inside are a Navy officer and a civilian wearing a hard hat.

In an aerial photo of USS *Kidd* taken around 1954, several changes are noticeable compared to her appearance in 1951. Among these are the removal of the gallery of three 20 mm guns and their splinter shield on the fantail, the removal of the 20 mm gun gallery on the main deck adjacent to the aft smokestack, the addition of a new platform with diagonal braces on the rear of the aft smokestack, and the removal of the 36-inch searchlights and their platforms from the forward smokestack.

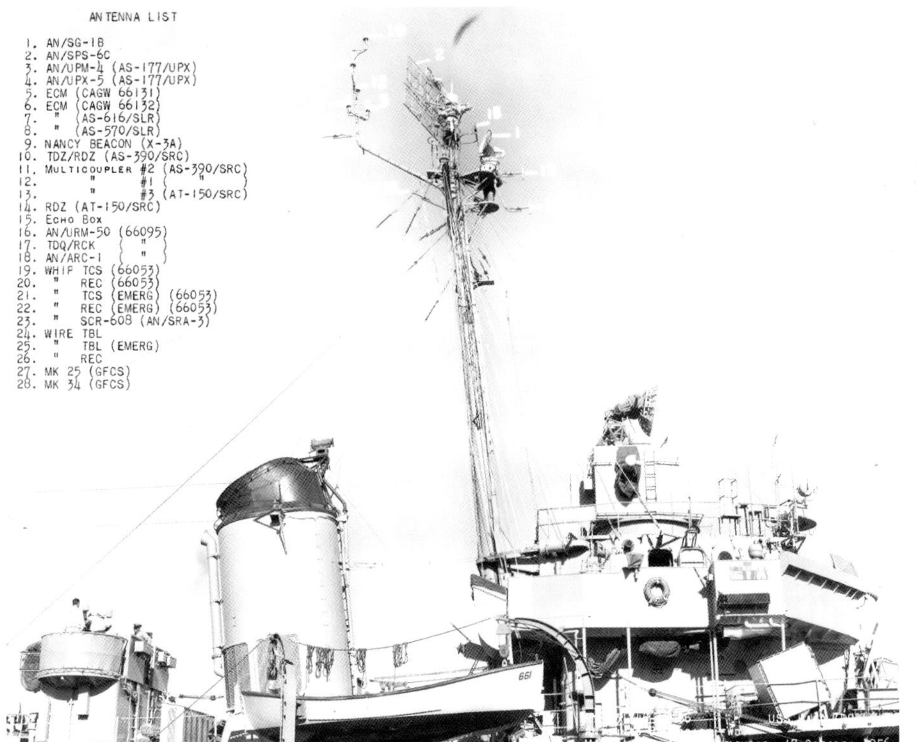

A photograph taken on October 16, 1956, documents the electronic equipment on the foremast, comprising a variety of radar and communications antennas. The principal radar antennas on the mast at this time were the AN/SPS-6C air-search radar at the top, and the AN/SG-1B surface-search radar to the lower front of the air-search antenna.

USS *Kidd* is underway on the high seas on May 28, 1957, sporting the postwar Haze Gray camouflage scheme with large, white ship's number, shadowed with black, on the bow. On the center of the bridge are a canvas sunscreen and a glass windshield. On the front of the superstructure deck, two 7.2-inch Hedgehog launchers along with ready-ammunition lockers had been installed; the ones on the starboard side are in view below the bridge. The Hedgehog was an array of spigot mortars that fired forward-launched antisubmarine projectiles.

The port side of USS *Kidd* is seen in another May 28, 1957, photograph. The 7.2-inch Hedgehog launchers and ready-ammunition lockers on the port side of the superstructure deck are visible below the bridge. A blast shield is above the mount captain's hatch on the roof of the number 1 5-inch/38-caliber gun mount, to protect the mount captain from blast from superfiring from the number 2 5-inch gun.

After the Korean War and continuing until the end of the 1950s, USS *Kidd* operated in the Pacific in an antisubmarine capacity. Here, *Kidd* is in a harbor at an unidentified site in the Pacific around 1958. By now, the Mk. 12/22 fire-control radar antenna on top of the Mk. 37 director had been replaced by a Mk. 25 parabolic dish antenna.

In an undated photograph, USS *Kidd* is steaming in close formation along the starboard side of the attack transport USS *Francis Marion* (APA-249). The photo dates to sometime between *Francis Marion*'s commissioning in July 1961 and *Kidd*'s decommissioning in June 1964.

USS *Kidd* appears in a postwar paint scheme of Haze Gray on all vertical surfaces, Deck Blue on horizontal surfaces, and large ship's number, white with black shadowing, on the bow. Kidd *served* several tours off Korea during the Korean War. *USS Kidd collection*

CHAPTER 3

Museum Ship

On December 1, 1974, USS *Kidd* was stricken from the navy list. Her age and equipment were such that she was no longer fit for service. While thirty-two of her Fletcher-class siblings had been transferred to allied navies, most had been consigned to the scrappers. *Kidd* was set aside for possible donation for preservation. This was in large part due to efforts of Harold Monning, who served aboard her during World War II, and the shipmates of the DesRon 48 Reunion Association.

In October 1979, through the additional efforts of Congressman W. Henson Moore, Governor Edwin Edwards, who appointed the Louisiana Naval War Memorial Commission, and the citizens of Louisiana, the Navy agreed to transfer *Kidd* to the state for use as a memorial honoring the state's veterans.

From the historical perspective, *Kidd*, among the handful (four) of surviving Fletcher-class destroyers, most nearly represented the World War II configuration of the ship, even retaining her World War II–era single-pole mast (the other ships had more-modern masts installed).

The decision was made to, as much as practicable, return the ship to her configuration of V-J Day. Therefore, the Navy was contracted to replace the 1950s-era "hedgehog" antisubmarine projectors mounted forward of the bridge with two twin 40 mm gun mounts. Fletcher-class destroyer USS *Caperton*, DD-650, also lying in reserve in Philadelphia but consigned for final use as a target ship, was cannibalized for some of the components missing from *Kidd*. Those parts included the quintuple Mk. 14 21-inch torpedo tubes, as well as a Mk. 27 torpedo director, two Mk. 63 gun directors, and a boat boom.

On May 23, 1982, *Kidd* arrived under tow in Baton Rouge, with throngs of people lining the banks of the Mississippi to welcome the veteran warship to her final home port. A special cradle was built, which allows the ship to ride the seasonal rise and fall of the Mississippi River; half of the year she floats, and the other half she rests high and dry on the cradle. Following extensive cleaning and painting, as well as minor modifications to accommodate the public, on August 27, 1983, *Kidd* was opened to the public.

Although, as previously stated, *Kidd* was largely intact when she arrived, her staff and volunteers continued the search for various missing items, to more completely return the destroyer to her August 1945 configuration.

In 1984, the Dutch navy donated two twin 20 mm gun mounts, two Mk. 16 "K-gun" depth charge projectors, and twelve 20 mm magazine drums. The Navy allowed *Kidd* personnel to remove parts from destroyer minelayer USS *Tolman* (DM-28), which had been decommissioned in 1947 and was slated to be used as a target ship. From *Tolman*, *Kidd* received four more "K-guns," a 36" searchlight and platform, and a Mk. 12/22 fire-control radar antenna, as well as several smaller items. Responding to a 1995 appeal from *Kidd*, the Turkish navy donated twelve Mk. 9 depth charges.

In 2018, Kidd was used as the set for the Tom Hanks movie *Greyhound*, portraying the fictional destroyer USS *Keeling*.

Today, resplendent in her Measure 22 camouflage and with the Jolly Roger flying high, and sporting a pirate on her funnel, *Kidd* welcomes veterans and visitors and serves as a memorial to those who sacrificed so much to preserve liberty.

USS *Kidd* (DD-661) is a member of the Fletcher class of destroyers, the largest class of destroyers in the US Navy in World War II. It is one of only three Fletcher-class destroyers on exhibit in the United States, the other two being USS *Cassin Young* (DD-793) and USS *The Sullivans* (DD-537).

The destroyer *Kidd* rests in Baton Rouge, Louisiana, as the centerpiece of the USS *Kidd* Veterans Memorial. She is said to be the only destroyer in the world restored to resemble her appearance and configuration in World War II. The ship is painted in a Measure 22 camouflage scheme, similar to the one she wore during 1945, with Haze Gray (5-H) on vertical surfaces down to the lowest point on the main deck, and Navy Blue (5-N) from that point down to the black boot topping near the waterline.

The starboard side of the bow is shown close-up. The ship carried two Baldt patent anchors, one on each side. The shank of the anchor, when raised as shown in this photo, fits in the hawsepipe, leaving the flukes (or hooks at the bottom) exposed.

Kidd presents her bow, forward single 5-inch/38-caliber gun mounts, superstructure, and foremast to view. The 5-inch/38-caliber gun mounts (properly referred to as such, and not as turrets) were numbered forward to aft. Hence, the two seen in this photo are mounts number 1 and, facing to starboard, number 2. The black band around the hull extending above and below the waterline is the boot topping, a gloss-black paint intended to hide the oily deposits that would cling to the hull in a harbor.

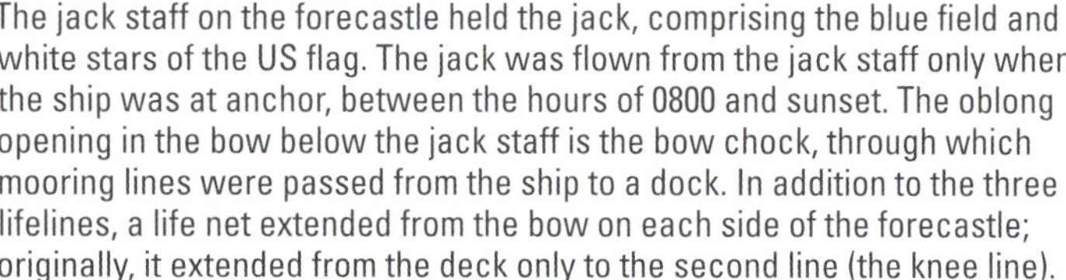

The jack staff on the forecastle held the jack, comprising the blue field and white stars of the US flag. The jack was flown from the jack staff only when the ship was at anchor, between the hours of 0800 and sunset. The oblong opening in the bow below the jack staff is the bow chock, through which mooring lines were passed from the ship to a dock. In addition to the three lifelines, a life net extended from the bow on each side of the forecastle; originally, it extended from the deck only to the second line (the knee line).

The main deck is viewed from the forecastle, showing the anchor chains. Affixed to the chains are stoppers, safety devices shackled to the deck and fastened to the anchor chains with pelican hooks, to secure the anchor chains in a stationary position when the anchors are raised. Aft of the anchor chains, at the centerline of the deck, is the windlass. Abreast of the windlass on each side of the deck is a 10-inch bitt, used in mooring the ship. The deck was fabricated mostly from 20-pound special-treatment steel (STS).

The hawsepipes are shown, with the tops of the port and starboard anchors visible in them. The pelican hooks that secure the stoppers to the anchor chains are in view; the chain running parallel to the port anchor chain is the port stopper.

The hawsepipes as viewed from the forecastle are shown in detail. D-shaped grilles cover the forward ends of the hawse holes, to prevent crewmen from stepping into them. A single bitt is designed into the aft outboard corner of each hawsepipe.

The port anchor is shown, providing a good view of its bottom. A reinforcing plate is attached to the hull, starting at the hawsepipe and extending downward. This protected the thin shell, or outer skin, of the hull from being damaged by the anchor as it was raised.

The stoppers for the anchor chains are shown close-up. Turnbuckles are incorporated into the stoppers, to enable snugging them once attached to the anchor chains. In the background are the chain-pipe end covers, attached to the deck with toggle bolts.

The windlass comprises an upper capstan for pulling on mooring lines, and a lower wildcat, which acts like a drive sprocket on the anchor chains, raising or lowering the anchor. The windlass's electrohydraulic driver was in the windlass room, one deck below.

The wing nuts and toggle bolts that hold the chain-pipe end covers in place are called dogs. The starboard anchor chain is routed around the windlass and down the starboard chain pipe, while the port anchor chain goes straight down into the port chain pipe.

The stoppers are fastened to pad eyes attached to the deck inboard of each chain pipe end cover. The stoppers took a great deal of stress off the windlass, which otherwise would have to support the considerable weight of the anchor and chain.

Aft of the windlass are, *to the left*, under a canvas cover, the windlass drum switch, and, *right*, the windlass brake wheel. Using these controls, a crewman on deck could operate the raising and lowering of the anchor. The welded joints of the deck plates are visible.

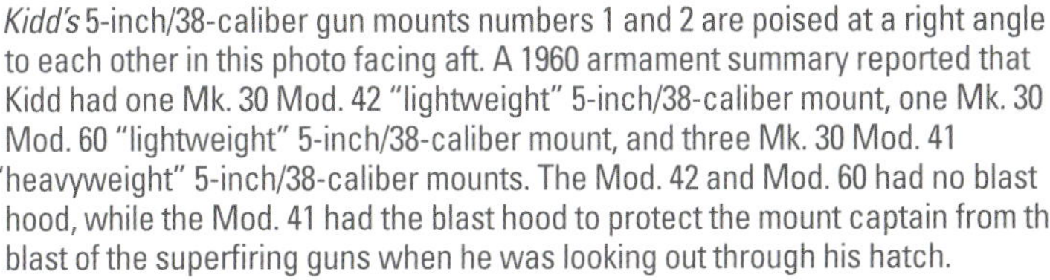

Kidd's 5-inch/38-caliber gun mounts numbers 1 and 2 are poised at a right angle to each other in this photo facing aft. A 1960 armament summary reported that Kidd had one Mk. 30 Mod. 42 "lightweight" 5-inch/38-caliber mount, one Mk. 30 Mod. 60 "lightweight" 5-inch/38-caliber mount, and three Mk. 30 Mod. 41 "heavyweight" 5-inch/38-caliber mounts. The Mod. 42 and Mod. 60 had no blast hood, while the Mod. 41 had the blast hood to protect the mount captain from the blast of the superfiring guns when he was looking out through his hatch.

Mounts 1 and 2 are viewed from closer, showing the open front of the blast hood on the roof of mount 1. A buckler, also called a blast bag, is fitted over the barrel of the 5-inch gun to provide a seal between the gun and the front of the gunhouse.

The gunhouse, also called the shield, was formed of 0.25-inch-thick steel. Doors to protect windows for the trainer (*left*) and pointer (*right*) are at the top of the photo. Visible below the shield and attached to the deck is the base ring stand, which supported the mount.

In addition to the windows, oblong doors cover the openings for the pointer's and the trainer's telescopes. The pointer elevated the mount, and the trainer traversed it when the mount was under local control: that is, not under the control of a director.

As viewed from behind, the blast hood was a shell designed to protect the gun mount captain from concussion from mount 2's gun when it superfired. Superfiring is when a higher gun fires over a lower gun mount. The cylinder is a lift assist for the hatch.

The blast hood on mount 1 is at the center. To get a clear view of the action outside, the gun mount captain would open his hatch and observe through the front of the hood, using the ring-type open sight to track targets. At the top is the Mk. 37 director.

Protruding from the bottom of the rear side of the shield of 5-inch mount number 1 is the case deflector door, where spent 5-inch cartridge cases were ejected from the gunhouse. On the side of the shield is the starboard hatch and door, with a step below it.

An aft port view of 5-inch mount number 1 shows that side's hatch and door with four locking handles, as well as details of the blast hood, with its external ribbing. A ladder for accessing the roof of the shield was provided on the port side of some of these mounts.

Inside the superstructure below 5-inch gun mount 2 is that mount's ammunition-handling room. In that room, ammunition brought up by hoist from a powder magazine and a projectile magazine on the third platform is prepared for hoisting up to the mount.

The relative positions of 5-inch mount number 2 on the superstructure deck and mount 1 on the main deck are illustrated. To the left is the forward starboard twin 40 mm gun mount, with the bridge and pilothouse one level above and the Mk. 37 director at the top.

The gun mount captain's hatch on 5-inch mount number 1 is on the port side of the roof, while the same hatch on 5-inch mount 2 is on the starboard side. On the rear of mount 2, above the case deflector door, are an electric bell and a louvered vent.

On the front of the first level of the superstructure are a fire hose reel, water lines, valves, and hoses. Above the red water lines is a basket that held a floating life net. A number of these baskets were mounted around the ship, and should the ship sink, the nets would float to the surface, giving crewmen something to hold on to and stay together until rescued. On the deck to the bottom right, with a canvas cover over it, is a watertight hatch. Originally, a 20 mm gun was mounted on each side of the superstructure deck aft of 5-inch gun mount 2, but near the end of the war, twin 40 mm mounts and new splinter shields replaced them.

The floater net rack, hoses, and reels to the front of the superstructure are viewed close-up. The door leads into a fan room and equipment space; there is one such room on each side of the superstructure here, outboard of the 5-inch ammunition-handling room.

The floater net rack, complete with a net inside, is viewed from the superstructure deck. By nature, a destroyer could not hold enough boats and life rafts to save the entire crew if the ship were sunk; floater nets could preserve lives until a rescue craft arrived.

The 5-inch gun mount number 2 is viewed from the level above the pilothouse. On a detachable pole on the roof is an anchor light. The roof, as well as the decks, are painted Deck Blue (20-B), in accordance with Measure 22 camouflage instructions.

Near the aft starboard corner of the roof of 5-inch gun mount number 2 is the gun mount captain's ring-type open sight, aft of which is his hatch. Protruding above the rear of the hatch is the hatch door stop. A close view of the anchor light is also provided.

The 40 mm gun barrels are shown close-up. These barrels had a definite life span, since the bores would wear out after prolonged firing, so it was necessary to change them after they had met their limit. To the upper left is part of the port forward 40 mm gun mount.

The 5-inch gun mount 2 is viewed from its starboard side. Above the side door is a rain deflector. On the superstructure deck, along with several poles, are two spare 40 mm gun barrels. To the right is the front of the starboard 40 mm mount's splinter shield.

Twin 40 mm gun mounts flank the front of the superstructure on the superstructure deck. The door leads into a ventilation fan room that also served as a 20 mm ammunition clipping and storage room and a shelter for the crews of these two 40 mm gun mounts.

Some of the forward part of the superstructure is viewed from starboard. At the top is the pilothouse, surrounded on the sides and front by the navigating bridge. The top of the forward portion of the navigating bridge has a venturi windshield, which deflected strong winds from blowing in the faces of personnel on the bridge. Just aft of the venturi windshield is the ship's kill board, enumerating enemy targets destroyed. Above the kill board is a pelorus, an instrument for taking bearings. Aft of the pelorus is a 12-inch signal lamp. Two life rafts are present.

The starboard forward twin 40 mm gun mount and, above it, the starboard wing of the bridge are viewed facing aft from the main deck. Near the outer side of the bridge is a Mk. 51 director, which normally controlled the 40 mm mount seen in this view.

The forward starboard twin 40 mm gun mount is viewed from the side. The pointer elevated the guns when the mount was under "local control" (i.e., not under control of the director); the pointer's seat, ring-and-bead sight, and control handwheel are in view.

The twin 40 mm gun mounts on USS *Kidd* were the Mk. 1 Mod. 2 type, incorporating two Bofors guns on a common carriage. This mount and the one adjacent to it were installed during a refitting completed in February 1945, replacing three 20 mm gun mounts.

The port forward twin 40 mm gun mount is shown, including the trainer's seat, sight, control handwheel, and footrests. The trainer traversed the mount when it was under local control. On top of the gun receivers is a cover over the automatic loading hoppers.

In a front view of the port forward twin 40 mm guns, the pointer's and trainer's sights are mounted on a crossbar fitted with curved guards for the rather fragile sights. Originally, the insides of the splinter shields for the 40 mm guns had racks for ready ammunition.

The 40 mm gun barrels are water cooled; the two rubber hoses along the gun are coolant hoses. Above the hoses is the starboard trunnion. Below the gun's receiver is the elevating arc, and to the left is a lever for manually preparing the gun for firing.

The structure of the bulwark of the splinter shield of the forward port twin 40 mm gun mount is illustrated, along with the design of the frame under the mount's platform. Triangular stiffeners were welded at intervals around the splinter shield.

The trainer's seat and controls are viewed from aft. Like the pointer, the trainer used his handwheel only when the mount was under manual, unpowered, control. The instrument atop the training-gear column at the center is the train correspondence indicator.

The tops of twin 40 mm guns are shown, including the recoil springs around the bases of the barrels and cooling-water hoses. To the bottom right are the two upper doors of the gun receivers, or housings, with locking levers to the fronts of the doors.

The forward starboard twin 40 mm gun mount is viewed from behind. At the rear of the loaders' platform is a coolant tank; a pump circulated water from it to the guns. The curved fixtures to the front of the tank are spent-casing chutes.

A platform for the loaders is at the rear of the twin 40 mm gun mount. The platform floor has antiskid tread. A safety rail is installed on the platform. At the center rear of the platform are four wooden poles that screw together to form a barrel-cleaning rod.

The part of the superstructure aft of the starboard forward 40 mm gun mount contains Radio Central, the main radio compartment on USS *Kidd*, and the chart room. Below the stowed fire hose is a 40 mm ammunition tank, or container.

On the top level is the Mk. 37 director and, below it, the pilothouse and navigating bridge, with part of the foremast to the left. Arrayed on the bridge are two 12-inch signal lamps, a torpedo director under a canvas cover, a pelorus, and a Mk. 51 director.

The Mk. 37 director controlled the operation of USS *Kidd*'s 5-inch/38-caliber mounts when those mounts were under automatic control. Crewmen in the director visually tracked targets with telescopes, sending that information to a Mk. 1A analog fire-control computer linked to a stable element (a device that compensates for the pitch and roll of the ship) in the interior communications and plotting room (IC-PLOT). The computer generated firing solutions for the 5-inch guns. On top of the director is a Mk. 12 fire-control radar antenna, which greatly increased the ability of the director to acquire and track targets. To the starboard side of that antenna is a late World War II modification: an "orange peel" parabolic antenna for the Mk. 22 radar, a height-finding set that enhanced the Mk. 12's ability to track low-angle targets.

The Mk. 37 director and Mk. 12 / Mk. 22 radar antennas are viewed from the front. On the front of the director are three windows, covers folded down, for, left to right, the trainer, pointer, and control officer. On the forward part of the roof, painted Deck Blue, are also three spotting hatches for the three men. The control officer had command of the director and designated targets by using a slewing scope. The pointer kept the horizontal crosshair of the director's sight on the target, and the trainer kept the vertical crosshair on target. Also in the director were a rangefinder operator (the rangefinder is the tubes protruding from the sides of the director), several talkers, and a radar operator.

The Mk. 12 radar was effective against air and surface targets. The radar operator selected targets and fed that information to the trainer and pointer, who aimed the director accordingly; close cooperation between these three crewmen was required.

The starboard side of the rangefinder protrudes from the side of the Mk. 37 director, with a boot (or bloomer) sealing the gap between the rangefinder and the director's housing. Handrails, footrails, and the ladder enabled men to work on the exterior of the director.

The frame of the Mk. 12 radar antenna on top of the Mk. 37 director is viewed from aft. During the antikamikaze action of April 11, 1945, this director was used so intensively that systems broke down, forcing the director crew to revert to manual control.

At the top of the foremast is a late-war SC-4 air-search radar antenna with a smaller, rectangular BL-5 interrogator antenna on top of it. Below the SC-4 is an SG-1 surface-search radar antenna. A BK "ski pole" transponder antenna is at each end of the yardarm.

Towering above the Mk. 37 director is the foremast. The main purpose of this mast on USS *Kidd* was to provide an elevated structure for mounting radar and radio antennas. The yardarm on the mast also served for flying signal flags from the halyards.

With the navigating bridge in the foreground, the Mk. 37 director and the foremast loom in the background. As built, USS *Kidd* had a small platform for a 20 mm gun in front of the center of the bridge, but this was later removed during a refitting.

In addition to the radar antennas, the foremast and yardarm provide mounting locations for numerous radio-transmitting and radio-receiving antennas. USS *Kidd* was officially sanctioned to fly the Jolly Roger pirate flag from the mast during World War II.

On the starboard side of the navigating bridge are, left to right, a Mk. 51 director, for controlling the starboard forward 40 mm gun mount, with a platform made of grating; a pelorus, for taking bearings; a speaking tube; and a 12-inch signal lamp.

The 12-inch signal lamp on the starboard side of the navigating bridge is shown close-up from behind. On the rear of the light are the General Electric logo and a handle. On the left side of the light housing is the handle that controls the shutters for signaling.

As viewed from the starboard side of the navigating bridge, the Mk. 51 director is in the center, with the pelorus, the searchlight, and a spotting telescope to the right. These instruments were also mounted in the same order on the port side of the navigating bridge.

At the center, on the starboard side of the navigating bridge, is a spotting telescope. Aft of it, to the right, is a Mk. 27 torpedo director with a canvas cover over it. There were two torpedo directors on the ship, on each side of the navigating bridge.

Another 12-inch signal lamp is aft of the torpedo director on the starboard side of the navigating bridge. Like the forward searchlight on this bridge, it is on a yoke mount on a swing arm. Below is a motorized whaleboat.

On the port side of the navigating bridge is situated a Mk. 51 director. Under cover is the director's Mk. 14 lead-computing sight. A ring-and-bead sight is also mounted. The mount was aimed using the handlebars; above the right grip is a counterweight.

This is the front of the bridge, facing starboard. In the foreground are spotting binoculars on a pedestal mount. The handle on the trunnion of the binoculars controlled their elevation. The yoke of the mount could be raised for viewing at higher angles.

Under cover to the left of the Mk. 51 director is a pelorus, which incorporates both a gyrocompass repeater, displaying readings from the ship's master gyrocompass, and a superimposed movable vane, used to establish both true and relative bearings on objects.

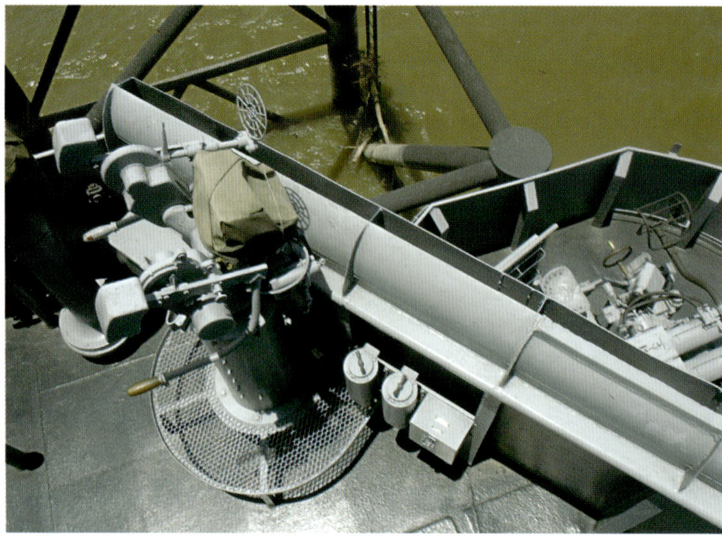

The port Mk. 51 director on the navigating bridge is viewed from above. One deck below it is the gun mount this Mk. 51 director controlled. When the operator kept the reticle of the director's Mk. 14 sight on the target, the sight computed the lead for the guns.

On the port wing of the bridge is a spotting telescope (*center*). To the left is a Mk. 27 torpedo director under cover. This unit comprised a stand, telescope, and case containing equipment to calculate a torpedo-firing solution and transmit it to the torpedo tubes.

The port wing of the navigating bridge is observed from atop the pilothouse. Adjacent to the pelorus is a speaking tube, through which voice messages could be sent to other parts of the ship. The cap of the tube is open. To the left is a 12-inch signal lamp.

The aft part of the bridge is the signal bridge, the port corner of which is depicted. A 12-inch signal lamp is to the right, and a 36-inch searchlight is on the searchlight platform around the forward smokestack. To the bottom left is the signal flag bag.

The General Electric 12-inch signal lamp on the port wing of the navigating bridge is shown close-up. This light could be used for illuminating targets or objects at night, or as a day or night signaling device for tapping out messages in Morse code.

At the rear of the bridge is an inclined ladder down to the superstructure deck. To the left of the ladder is the lower part of the foremast. Two antenna trunks are to the left of the mast, and to the left of the antenna trunks is the port signal flag bag.

The aft corner of the port wing of the navigating bridge is viewed from above, with the torpedo director to the right. The port signal flag bag, to the left, and a similar flag bag on the opposite side of the bridge were storage bins for the ship's signal flags.

The lower part of the exposed portion of the foremast has a variety of electrical cables attached. The foundation of the mast is one level below, on the main deck. The door to the right provides access to Radio Central, the chart room, and the coding room.

The foremast is observed from its port side; it disappears down into a square-shaped opening in the superstructure deck, with guardrails and chains around it. In the background is the starboard whaleboat. A crew member who was present at this location at 1410 hours on April 11, 1945, would have witnessed a Japanese kamikaze plane bearing in at low level for the starboard side of the ship. The aircraft slammed into the hull below the location of this whaleboat, a few feet above the waterline, causing extensive damage and losses to the crew.

This view of the foremast was taken from atop the captain's sea cabin, in the aft part of the pilothouse structure. Alongside the mast is a vertical ladder. This provided access to the upper reaches of the foremast, since it was essential for crewmen to be able to repair and maintain the mast's rigging, radar and radio antennas, lights, and electrical systems. Arrayed around the foremast are various halyards for flying signal flags, stays for bracing the mast, and wire antennas and antenna leads. To the left, part of the forward smokestack is visible.

This photo, taken from the same position as the preceding view, shows the triangular platform surrounding the foremast to the rear of the roof of the pilothouse / sea cabin, with a vertical ladder to the side of the mast. In the background is the searchlight platform.

This is a communications panel on the level atop the pilothouse. In a rack on the panel is an M2 helmet. This type of helmet was used by "talkers," who relayed signals by telephone, and was extra large, to fit over a communications headset.

Mounted on the aft bulkhead of the pilothouse / sea cabin is the torpedo control panel, for remote firing from the bridge. This location is close to the torpedo directors. If necessary, crewmen stationed at the torpedo tubes could fire the torpedoes.

On each side of the front of the level above the pilothouse is a lookout's seat with a binoculars holder. Lookouts methodically searched for any enemy aircraft or ships that slipped through the ship's radar coverage. To the right is a signalman's platform.

This is on the port side of the superstructure deck, or 01 level, facing aft, with the outer bulkhead of Radio Central and a ventilation duct to the left. To the lower right are stowed life rafts, while at the top is the underside of the navigating bridge.

The lower part of the forward smokestack is viewed facing aft on the superstructure deck. The ship's two smokestacks directed fumes and vapors from the boilers up and away from the decks. A 20 mm ready-service ammunition box is in the center foreground.

The portside whaleboat is observed from above. Fitted over its forward half is a canopy. In the lower part of the photo is a brace that holds the top of the davit stationary. The 26-foot whaleboats aboard *Kidd* at the time of this writing were salvaged from the cruiser USS *Albany* (CA-123). A diesel motor powered a single propeller on these boats. The ship's original whaleboats were made of wood, a practice discontinued some sixty years ago; these examples are made of fiberglass. Each boat held twenty-five men.

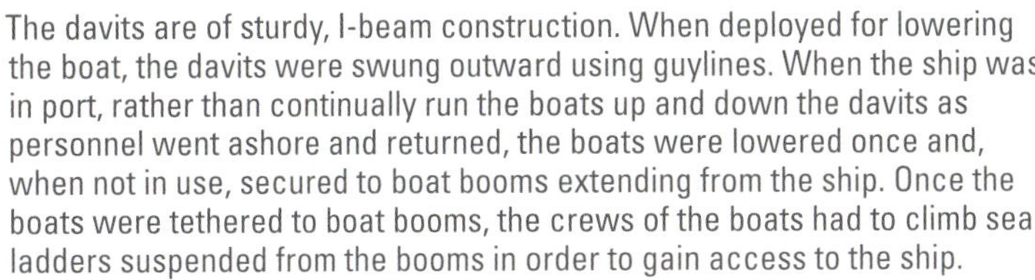

The davits are of sturdy, I-beam construction. When deployed for lowering the boat, the davits were swung outward using guylines. When the ship was in port, rather than continually run the boats up and down the davits as personnel went ashore and returned, the boats were lowered once and, when not in use, secured to boat booms extending from the ship. Once the boats were tethered to boat booms, the crews of the boats had to climb sea ladders suspended from the booms in order to gain access to the ship.

Attached to the davits are bumpers, against which the boats rest, to keep them from jarring against the davits as the ship pitches and rolls at sea. Each boat carried a crew of three: the coxswain, who steered the boat by using an old-fashioned tiller-and-rudder arrangement; the engineman; and the bow hook, who took care of mooring the boat and attaching and detaching the boat falls. The pipe structures in the background are not part of USS *Kidd* but are part of the docking system for the ship.

In a view of the whaleboat on the starboard side, the bow is to the left, and the cover for the diesel motor is toward the right. To the upper right are monkey ropes: bunched, knotted lines that personnel could grasp while standing up in the boat.

The whaleboat on the starboard side is viewed from aft and below, showing the propeller and rudder. Several different straps called grips are employed to secure the boat to the davit and are attached to clevises fastened to pad eyes on the side of the davit.

The aft part of the whaleboat and the aft starboard davit are depicted. The coxswain stood up on the platform with the guardrails in the stern and operated the tiller, directly connected to the top of the rudder. The engineman was positioned next to the engine to the left.

The whaleboat suspended from the starboard davits is viewed from ashore. On the line connecting the tops of the davits are hanks of ropes. These were used to allow eight men at a time to descend down to the boat. The whaleboats would be too heavy and unstable to lower to the sea if they were loaded to their full capacity of twenty-two men, including two crew while being lowered. Below the boat is a life raft. A spotlight is mounted under the bridge, below the top of the forward davit.

Features above the main deck from the forward superstructure to the forward smokestack are emphasized in this view of the starboard side of USS *Kidd*. To the upper right is the Mk. 37 director, with Mk. 12 and Mk. 22 radar antennas on top. Below the director is the pilothouse and bridge. The forward starboard twin 40 mm gun mount is to the lower right. Partway up the forward smokestack is the searchlight platform. Below the whaleboat on the main deck is a bulwark with a door through its forward face. Scuppers at the bottom of the bulwark allow water that washed on deck to flow back out.

Although the ship was named for RAdm. Isaac Kidd, the original crew assembled when the ship was commissioned, known as plank owners, obtained official sanction to adopt the famous pirate of the seventeenth century, Captain William Kidd, as their mascot. A painting of Captain Kidd similar to the current one decorated each side of the forward smokestack dating from the ship's earliest service. The ship also enjoyed the nickname "the Pirate of the Pacific." The small Jolly Roger pirate flag the ship was authorized to fly from its halyards was also in this spirit.

The matte-black caps on the smokestacks are a post–World War II addition and are not part of the official Measure 22 camouflage. Other than the matte-black tops of the smokestacks, the rest of the structures seen in this photo are painted Haze Gray, in accordance with the Measure 22 camouflage scheme the ship wore during 1945, the last year of World War II. The searchlight platform is attached to the front of the forward smokestack and supports two 36-inch searchlights. Guardrails are around the platform, and a canvas windbreak is lashed to the rails on the port side of the platform. On the side of the smokestack aft of the searchlight platform is a bin for a floating life net.

The 26-foot whaleboat on the port side of USS *Kidd* is viewed from astern. To the upper right of the boat is the curved shape of the portside signal flag bag. To the right are a floating life net basket and, below it, two ventilators for the smokestack.

The front of the lower part of the forward smokestack and the tubular supports for the searchlight platform are viewed from the signal bridge. The metal plate on the ladder in front of the smokestack is not original but intended to deter climbers.

The upper part of the forward smokestack is viewed from the bridge. A small service platform with guardrails is toward the top of the stack. To the port side of the service platform is a vertical ladder, providing access to the upper part of the smokestack. Footrails and handrails around the upper part of the funnel allowed crewmen to work on the structure. The shell of the main part of the smokestack below the top section has a very pronounced texture.

Supporting the small service platform toward the top of the forward smokestack are braces formed from angle irons. Located just above the front of the forward smokestack are a whistle and a siren. Covers made of fine netting are fitted over them to keep out insects and foreign matter. Also in view is the port wing of the searchlight platform, with the 36-inch searchlight, pointing forward, behind the canvas windscreen lashed to the guardrails.

The starboard wing of the searchlight platform is observed from atop the pilothouse. The 36-inch searchlights were illuminated by high-intensity carbon arcs, focused by a 36-inch parabolic reflector. These searchlights could be operated by their crew or could be operated remotely by the Mk. 37 director in unison with the 5-inch/38-caliber gun mounts. Searchlights were useful in nighttime battles, to illuminate targets and identify them as enemy.

On outrigger mounts on each side of the forward smokestack are antennas that resemble a segment of a spoked wheel. These represent BLR "sword" electronic-countermeasure (ECM) antennas installed on the ship during her refitting in the summer of 1945.

The BLR "sword" ECM antennas on the forward smokestack are viewed from another angle. ECM equipment on the ship was designed to detect and jam enemy communications and radar. At the top of the smokestack are the whistle and siren.

The starboard 36-inch searchlight is viewed close-up. To the front of the light's drum is a door comprising a hinged frame and a clear, convex lens. An operator's seat is to the side of the base of the mount. Powered mechanisms for aiming the light were included.

The US Navy's 36-inch searchlights produced a narrow, nonflickering light beam of bluish-white color. They were required to function in all weather conditions, and dependability even during hard service was a prime consideration.

The forward smokestack is viewed from below, showing the arrangement of the two ventilators on its lower part, the searchlight platform, the floater net basket above the ventilators, and the ECM antenna. Attached to the upper rim of the floater net basket is a nonoriginal lighting fixture. Rising above the searchlight platform is the foremast. The Captain Kidd artwork is not painted directly onto the smokestack but is a painted cutout fastened to the smokestack. The vertical tube at the rear of the smokestack with the flared opening is the steam pipe.

As built, on USS *Kidd's* superstructure deck between the two smokestacks was a five-tube, 21-inch torpedo mount, with a similar mount aft of the aft smokestack. During the ship's refitting and repair following the April 1945 kamikaze attack, the forward torpedo mount was removed, as were the two twin 40 mm gun mounts to the sides of the aft smokestack, and quadruple (quad) 40 mm gun mounts were installed on new mounts slightly forward of the aft smokestack. Also, new directors for the Mk. 63 Gunfire Control System (GFCS) were mounted on the platform forward of the quad 40 mm mounts.

On the port side of the main deck below the platform for the Mk. 63 directors is the boat winch, which served to raise and lower the whaleboats on their davits. One winch served both boats, by means of ropes routed as necessary through blocks, or pulleys.

On top of this deckhouse installed in 1945 is a platform for the two directors of the Mk. 63 GFCS, which worked in unison with a radar antenna mounted on the associated quad 40 mm gun mount on either side of the superstructure deck, just aft of the platform.

The boat winch is shown with respect to other structures in its vicinity, facing aft. The structure with the orange life ring buoy is a deckhouse that contained radar equipment for the quad 40 mm gun mount directly above it. On the splinter shield of the gun mount is a rack for stowing crewmen's helmets, which they would wear when manning the guns for combat. The open door toward the left leads into the laundry, where crewmen worked tirelessly to wash, dry, and press clothing for the ship's crew.

The same deckhouse and director platform in the preceding photo is viewed from the superstructure deck, facing aft toward the quad 40 mm gun mount on the port side of the deck. Flanking the ladder are a ventilator, *left*, and a locker.

The front of the deckhouse is shown. To the left, the radar dish antenna on the starboard quad 40 mm mount was linked to the starboard director on the platform. Early versions of the Mk. 63 GFCS used the Mk. 51 director chassis with the Mk. 15 Mod. 12 gunsight.

The deckhouse and overhang of the director platform are viewed from the main deck, with the forward smokestack to the right and the aft smokestack to the left. A ventilation duct is at the aft corner of the deckhouse, and a light is mounted on its side.

Viewed from aft, the deckhouse between the smokestacks on the superstructure deck not only supported the platform for the Mk. 63 directors but also served as a ready-service ammunition room for the quad 40 mm guns on the superstructure deck.

On the superstructure deck immediately forward of the aft smokestack, a secondary conning station was added during USS *Kidd's* 1945 refitting at Hunters Point Naval Shipyard, San Francisco. A curved splinter shield is in front of the station.

The crew at the secondary conning station would communicate orders to crews in the engine rooms and steering-gear room to assist in controlling the ship in an emergency, using voice-powered telephone. A manual steering control was in the steering-gear room.

The secondary conning station was equipped with a binnacle, under a cover on top of the pedestal, with the iron correcting spheres projecting from its sides. This magnetic compass would allow an emergency conning crew to establish the course of the ship.

The quad 40 mm gun mounts and their directors replaced the forward torpedo tubes in the summer of 1945. This was in accordance with the Navy's response to the heavy kamikaze attacks of spring 1945: additional antiaircraft guns now took precedence over torpedoes.

The pointer's seat, footrests, and controls are on the left side of the quad 40 mm gun mount, as seen here. The pointer's right pedal was also the firing pedal. Next to the gun carriage is the elevation gear and handwheel, and to the upper left is the elevation arc.

On the right side of the quad 40 mm mount is the trainer's seat and controls. The handwheel is attached to the training-gear bracket assembly. Water hoses are attached to the gun barrels, and the recoil cylinders are missing from their brackets below the barrels.

In the quad 40 mm mount, two guns are mounted in each carriage. Two curved case chutes are behind each gun; spent cartridge cases ejected from the rear of the guns slide down these chutes and out through the lower ends of the chutes at the bottom left.

The radar dish antenna of the Mk. 63 GFCS is shown on its mount, most likely the Mk. 19 Mod. 1, on top of the two left guns in the port quad 40 mm gun mount. In the background, to the left of the smokestack, is the director for this gun mount.

The two quad 40 mm gun mounts are viewed from the starboard side of USS *Kidd*, showing their radar antennas from different perspectives. The Mk. 63 GFCS incorporated the Mk. 34 radar system.

Firefighting equipment is stored along the starboard superstructure on the main deck just aft of and below the quad 40 mm mount and below a floater-net basket. In the rack at left are cans of fire-extinguishing foam concentrate. The red tank is a foam dispenser.

The starboard quad 40 mm gun mount is viewed facing aft, with the 40 mm ready-service ammunition room to the right. In actual service, the splinter shield, or gun tub, of the 40 mm mount would have had storage racks for ready-ammunition clips.

The starboard quad 40 mm gun mount is viewed facing forward. To the rear of the mount is a platform with a guardrail for the loaders, who fed four-round clips of 40 mm ammunition into automatic feed hoppers on top of the guns as fast as they could.

The starboard quad 40 mm gun mount is viewed facing forward. To the rear of the mount is a platform with a guardrail for the loaders, who fed four-round clips of 40 mm ammunition into automatic feed hoppers on top of the guns as fast as they could.

The rear of the antenna for the Mk. 34 radar is shown. This antenna provided range information to the Mk. 63 GFCS. The operator of the GFCS was responsible for tracking the target with the Mk. 63 director's Mk. 14 gyro gunsight.

Aft of the starboard quad 40 mm gun mount, between the stanchions of the guardrail are two coolant water tanks for the guns, one tank per two guns. The automatic feeds atop the guns usually had these types of covers over them when not in use, to preserve them.

The starboard quad 40 mm gun mount is viewed from aft, with the aft smokestack to the left and the Mk. 63 director at the center. The director was located close to the gun mount to reduce parallax errors and was higher than the gun mount for better visibility.

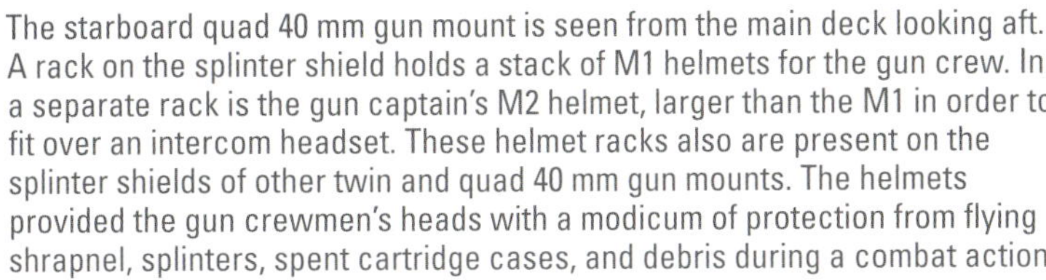

The starboard quad 40 mm gun mount is seen from the main deck looking aft. A rack on the splinter shield holds a stack of M1 helmets for the gun crew. In a separate rack is the gun captain's M2 helmet, larger than the M1 in order to fit over an intercom headset. These helmet racks also are present on the splinter shields of other twin and quad 40 mm gun mounts. The helmets provided the gun crewmen's heads with a modicum of protection from flying shrapnel, splinters, spent cartridge cases, and debris during a combat action.

The aft smokestack is observed from the starboard side of the ship. Originally, a twin 40 mm gun mount was to each side of this stack, and a platform for two directors for those mounts was partway up the smokestack, but the platform and gun mounts were removed during the refitting of the ship at Mare Island in the summer of 1945. Near the base of the smokestack are two ventilators. At the rear of the smokestack is the steam pipe, and attached to the base of the steam pipe is the battle flag staff, with two braces straddling the steam pipe.

The device at the top rear of the aft smokestack is a range light, which allowed ships behind to estimate the distance between the ships, for accurate station-keeping. Aft of the smokestack is the quintuple torpedo tube mount.

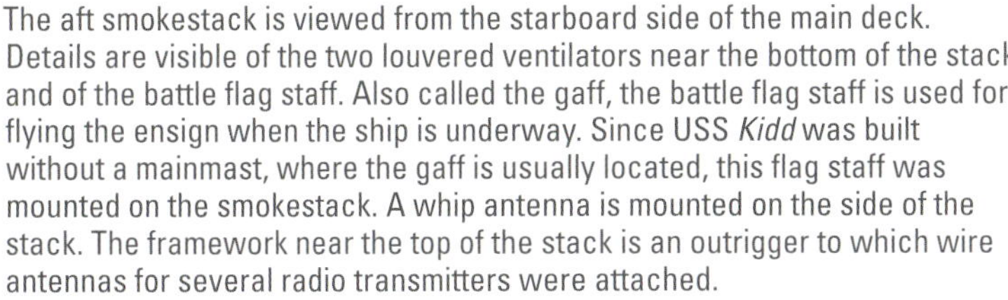

The aft smokestack is viewed from the starboard side of the main deck. Details are visible of the two louvered ventilators near the bottom of the stack and of the battle flag staff. Also called the gaff, the battle flag staff is used for flying the ensign when the ship is underway. Since USS *Kidd* was built without a mainmast, where the gaff is usually located, this flag staff was mounted on the smokestack. A whip antenna is mounted on the side of the stack. The framework near the top of the stack is an outrigger to which wire antennas for several radio transmitters were attached.

This view of the rear of the aft smokestack demonstrates how two separate lines coming out of the smokestack join together in an inverted Y at the bottom of the steam pipe. A flange at the top of that Y and a flange at the bottom of the steam pipe are fastened together with nuts and bolts. The steam pipe is fastened to the smokestack with U-shaped brackets. A cover has been fitted over the opening at the top of the steam pipe to keep out moisture and foreign objects. The mounting brackets for the whip antennas partway up the sides of the smokestack are visible.

In a view facing aft from the rear of the quad 40 mm gun tub on the port side of the superstructure deck, two twin 20 mm gun mounts are present on the main deck. These automatic Oerlikon guns were used for short-range antiaircraft defense. In the foreground is a floater net in its basket. Above it is the side of the base of the smokestack. Several torpedoes appear in their launching tubes aft of the smokestack. Farther aft is the number 3 5-inch/38-caliber gun mount, adjacent to which are two life rafts stowed on a rack over the main deck.

Each twin 20 mm Oerlikon gun is on a tripod stand with a pivoting carriage with a fixed trunnion height, meaning the gun carriage could not be raised when the gun was at a steep angle, as was the case with Navy pedestal mounts for the 20 mm Oerlikon gun.

Each 20 mm gun is fitted with a sixty-round ammunition magazine and a spent-case bag underneath the receiver. The gunner aimed the piece by using handlebars and shoulder rests that he was strapped into. The stands were installed with the base rings level.

The straps that held the gunner's shoulders tight to the shoulder rests are present on this twin 20 mm mount. Under cover is the gunsight; the Mk. 14 lead-computing gunsight was the type commonly used on this type of gun mount in the latter part of the war.

The twin 20 mm gun mounts on the starboard side are shown. When USS *Kidd* entered the service in 1943, she had ten single 20 mm gun mounts. These were reduced to seven in early 1945 and were replaced by seven twin 20 mm gun mounts in August 1945.

Extra magazines of 20 mm ammunition for quick retrieval by the loaders of the 20 mm guns were stored in ready-service ammunition boxes mounted on legs slightly above deck. The cover was secured in place by dogs: toggle bolts with ring-type nuts.

The two 20 mm guns are attached to a cradle with trunnions that fit into the carriage. The Mk. 14 gunsight is mounted on a saddle-type bracket attached to the carriage. The apparatus in the gap between the two plates of the gun shield is the gunsight power unit.

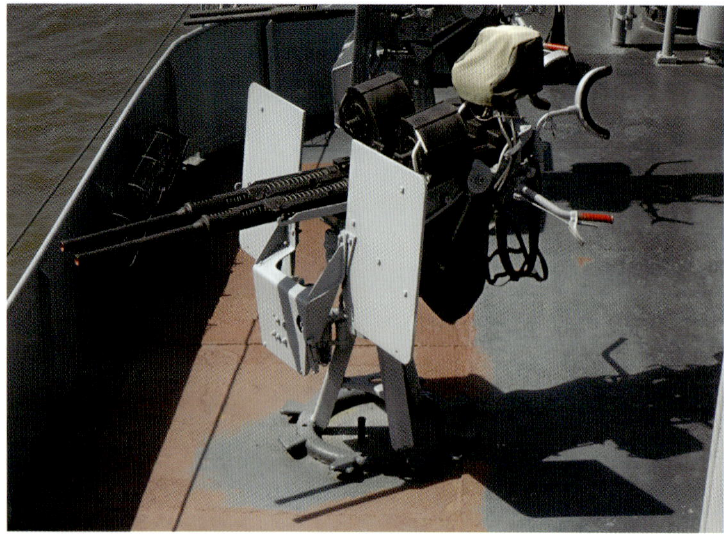

Two flat armor plates gave the 20 mm gun crew a degree of protection. Between the two plates is a projecting shield for the gunsight power unit. During battle, the loaders hustled to remove empty magazines and install loaded ones, each weighing 63 pounds.

A member of the gun crew manually set the target's range on the gunsight. The range-setting control is the large black knob toward the bottom of the side of the sight. The two smaller knobs on the side are the deflection spot control (*top*) and the elevation spot knob.

The Mk. 14 Mod. 6 lead-computing gunsights on *Kidd's* twin 20 mm gun mounts were designed to rapidly formulate a firing solution against short-range, fast-moving targets, calculating the necessary lead. The gunner tracked the target through the port in the top of the sight.

The front window is at the upper front of the sight. Inside the sight, between the front and rear windows, is a transparent elevation mirror upon which a reticle image is reflected to the gunner's eye. Two gyros form the heart of the complex inner mechanisms.

On the superstructure deck to the rear of the aft smokestack is a Mk. 15 Mod. 3 quintuple torpedo-tube mount. The mount was trained either to the starboard or the port side for launching the 21-inch torpedoes.

The extensions with the folded fronts forward of the tubes are the spoons, which engaged a lug on the aft part of the torpedo during firing, to keep the tail of the torpedo up and prevent the torpedo from hitting the ship as it was launched from the tube.

USS *Kidd*, as built, had a Mk. 14 quintuple-tube, 21-inch torpedo mount between the smokestacks and a Mk. 15 quintuple-tube, 21-inch torpedo mount in this position, the difference being the Mk. 15 had a blast shield for the operators, not present now.

The torpedoes were launched by igniting black-powder charges. The 21-inch-diameter, 24-foot-long Mk. 15 torpedo that this mount was designed for was powered by a steam-driven turbine, its warhead containing 800 pounds of high explosives.

Kidd was originally fitted with a conical blast shield like this one on USS *Cassin Young*, preserved in Boston. It was intended to protect the crew of the quintuple torpedo mount, stationed on top of the tubes, from the blast of the nearby 5-inch gun.

The quintuple torpedo mount's crew comprised the mount captain, trainer, and gyro setter, stationed atop the tubes. The controls seen here include the torpedo course indicator (*left*) and gyro-setter's controls (*right*). In the foreground are torpedo stops.

The dome-shaped fixtures at the rears of the torpedo tubes are impulse chambers. A black-powder cartridge called an impulse case was loaded into the rear of the chamber, and the cartridge was detonated electrically or by percussion, thus launching the torpedo.

A torpedo stop mechanism is seen close-up from the right side, with the others in the background. The purpose of the stop mechanism was to position the torpedo in the tube so the speed, depth, and gyro sockets on the torpedo were in proper alignment.

As viewed from the right side of the torpedo tubes are, *left to right*, the trainer's and gyro-setter's bench, the gyro-setter's controls, the trainer's handwheel, and torpedo course indicator. The mount captain was stationed on the deck to the left side of the mount.

On the starboard side of the quintuple torpedo-tube mount is a narrow catwalk (*left*), enabling the crew to pass from the forward part of the superstructure deck to the aft part. There was no corresponding catwalk on the port side of the torpedo-tube mount.

The torpedo tubes are seen from below. The cylinders attached to the bottoms of the doors are counterbalances. Several different models of door assemblies were used on destroyer torpedo tubes: these are the Mk. 8, with counterbalances and eight clamps.

The torpedo tubes are viewed from aft. The loading doors hinged at the bottoms and are secured shut with clamps. The impulse chambers on top of the tubes are visible. The gyro-setter's and the trainer's controls and indicators are on top of the tubes.

A retractable torpedo-handling crane and chain hoist are to the starboard rear of the torpedo tubes. To load a torpedo, a sling was fitted around its center of gravity, and the crane lifted it and inserted it partway into the tube; crewmen pushed it the rest of the way.

The loading crane is viewed from its front, fully retracted. The boom is of I-beam construction and is offset-mounted on the base, with a diagonal, tubular brace welded to the boom. The fixture bolted to the top of the crane is refueling-at-sea gear.

The loading crane is shown, facing forward. The refueling-at-sea fitting on top of the crane evidently was a postwar modification, since it does not appear on the cranes in photographs of USS *Kidd* after refitting and repairs at Mare Island, in August 1945.

A view forward from the starboard side of 5-inch/38-caliber gun mount number 3 includes the right rear of the quintuple 21-inch torpedo tubes, the starboard loading crane, two 20 mm gun mounts, the rear smokestack, and the starboard quad 40 mm gun mount.

On the main deck aft of the quintuple 21-inch torpedo tubes is a 5-inch loading machine. This device replicated the loading mechanism of the 5-inch/38-caliber guns and permitted their crews to hone their loading skills and teamwork outside of the close confines of the gun mount. The device is elevated and is viewed from the rear. On its right side is the powered rammer, to the left of which is the simulated breech and loading tray. To the left of the loading machine are a dummy fuse setter and a 5-inch projectile hoist.

Part of the 5-inch loading machine is visible from the starboard side of the main deck. The device could be elevated to allow crewmen to practice loading the piece at different angles; the elevating arc is visible below the loading machine and within the stand.

The front end of the 5-inch loading machine is observed from above, with the projectile deflector tray to the lower right. At the bottom center is the elevating gear and elevating handwheel. The rammer power unit is to the upper left on the loading machine.

Aft of the torpedoes and the 5-inch loading machine on the main-deck level is the aft deckhouse, viewed from the starboard side. This deckhouse contained, forward to aft, the ammunition-handling room for 5-inch/38-caliber gun mount number 3, the crew washroom, the crew lavatory and showers, the ammunition-handling room for 5-inch/38-caliber gun mount 4, and a fan room with lockers. Atop this deckhouse, between 5-inch/38-caliber gun mounts numbers 3 (*right*) and 4 (*left*), is a small deckhouse that contained a fan room, a shelter for the 40 mm gun crew, and storage space for 40 mm ready-service ammunition. Atop this small deckhouse is a twin 40 mm gun mount and its director.

Two life rafts are stowed on a rack adjacent to the aft deckhouse. These rafts were constructed of balsa-wood frames wrapped with doped canvas. At the bottom is a rack containing several mines. To the top left is the torpedo-handling crane.

Abeam each side of the aft deckhouse are three Mk. 6 depth-charge projectors and depth-charge ready racks. The ready racks seen here are loaded with Mk. 9 depth charges and two spare arbors (firing trays); not visible are the projectors aft of each ready rack.

The life rafts have platforms made of crisscrossed wooden slats, attached to the frame of the raft with webbing material. Also attached with the webbing material on the outsides of the frames are lines with floats, to which crewmen in the water could strap themselves.

These are the forward starboard Mk. 6 depth-charge projector (also called K-gun; a Mk. 6 depth charge is loaded) and ready rack. The davit was used for loading depth charges. An impulse charge loaded into the base of the projector served to propel the depth charge.

Seen from the top of the aft deckhouse, facing forward along the port side of the main deck, are the forward depth-charge ready rack (*lower left*), stowed life rafts, and two twin 20 mm gun mounts. To the right is the left rear corner of 5-inch/38-caliber gun mount number 3. The depth charges are the Mk. 9, which had a teardrop design to allow the weapon to sink faster. This type of depth charge also had fins on the base and a support ring around the nose. The Mk. 9 depth charge was filled with 200 pounds of TNT and was detonated by hydrostatic pressure at varying depths.

On the aft deckhouse is a stretcher called the Stokes litter. Its basket construction made it useful for carrying the wounded up and down ladders, and it also could be used to transfer the wounded to another ship by means of a highline stretched between the ships.

The front of 5-inch/38-caliber gun mount number 3 is viewed, with the upper deckhouse and director platform in the background. This gun mount, as well as the number 4 5-inch gun mount, have the two-panel roof with no blast hood.

The number 3 5-inch/38-caliber gun mount, the upper deckhouse, and the mainmast are observed from the starboard rear side of the torpedo tubes. The small mainmast was a summer 1945 modification that originally held two DBM radar direction finder antennas and an antenna for a TDY jamming device. A second dome-shaped DBM antenna originally was fitted on the small platform below and aft of the existing DBM antenna at the top of the mast. To the lower left is the refueling fixture bolted to the top of the torpedo-handling crane.

The number 3 5-inch/38-caliber gun mount on *Kidd* is viewed from below, showing part of the stand, the stationary assembly below the gunhouse that is bolted to the deck. The metal plate on the ladder is to prevent visitors from climbing it.

The mainmast installed on USS *Kidd* at the US Navy Shipyard at Hunters Point, California, in 1945 survived until at least the early 1950s, but by late in that decade it had been removed. The current mainmast apparently is a reconstruction of the 1945 one.

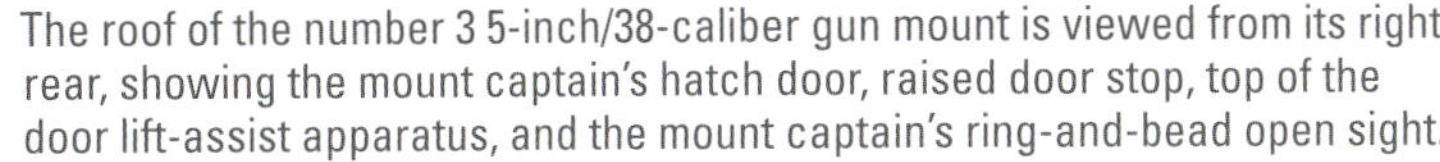

The roof of the number 3 5-inch/38-caliber gun mount is viewed from its right rear, showing the mount captain's hatch door, raised door stop, top of the door lift-assist apparatus, and the mount captain's ring-and-bead open sight.

The mount captain used the open sight when the 5-inch gun was under local or manual control, using hand cranks to align the sight with a target. Information on the sight's azimuth and elevation was transmitted to indicators at the pointer's and trainer's stations.

Beginning in 1944, USS *Kidd* wore camouflage scheme Measure 31/10D, which was designed especially for Fletcher-class destroyers. As with many official Navy camo schemes, there was minor variation from ship to ship, and the starboard bow stripe on *Kidd* was markedly different from that of the others. Prior to the application of the 31/10D scheme, she wore Measure 21, which consisted of overall 5-N Navy Blue with horizontal surfaces in 20-B Deck Blue. Between December 1944 and February 1945, the ship was in overhaul and emerged wearing Measure 22, featuring 5-H Haze Gray vertical surfaces but for a 5-N Navy Blue Band around the hull—the scheme in which the ship was preserved as of 2021, and as depicted on the front cover. After World War II and until her restoration, she had Haze Gray vertical surfaces overall, as seen on the rear cover of this book.

The deckhouse between 5-inch/38-caliber gun mounts numbers 3 (*right*) and 4 (*left*), viewed from the starboard side, showing the lower part of the mainmast and the platform on top of the deckhouse for a twin 40 mm gun mount and, on a small, raised platform, the director for the 40 mm gun mount. This director was not enclosed in a tub or splinter shield, but often a canvas windscreen would be lashed to the guardrails on the platform. A spotlight on a flexible mount is attached to the bulwark of the gun platform, and a davit for hoisting ammunition and supplies is next to the midsection of the deckhouse.

At the forward end of the platform for the twin 40 mm gun mount is a Mk. 51 director, which controlled the adjacent 40 mm guns. The pedestal and cradle of the director are present, but the Mk. 14 gunsight normally mounted on it is not installed. The two block-shaped objects projecting from the cradle are counterweights. Forward of the director is the lower part of the mainmast; at the top is a replica of a TDY radio-jamming antenna, part of the ship's electronic-countermeasures system installed in the summer of 1945. Outriggers provide attachment points for stays for the upper part of the mast.

The pointer's ring-and-bead sight and guard and the sight bracket on the aft twin 40 mm gun mount are shown. These were painted matte black to minimize glare. To the left are the recoil springs. The elevating arc is visible below the guns.

In a view of the carriage of the aft twin 40 mm gun mount, the pointer's elevation gear and elevating hand crank are toward the right. The mechanisms of this gun mount incorporated a maze of linkages, gear boxes, wiring, lines, and other fixtures.

The starboard side of the deckhouse between 5-inch/38-caliber gun mounts 3 and 4 is viewed from the main deck, facing forward. In the foreground is a spotlight, and forward of it is a floating-net basket. Depth-charge-handling davits are to the right.

The aft K-gun, or Mk. 6 depth-charge projector, on the starboard side of the main deck is loaded with a Mk. 9 depth charge. The base of the depth charge is in view, showing the eight stabilizing fins and rear ring. More Mk. 9 depth charges are in the rack.

Along the starboard bulkhead of the first level of the aft deckhouse are stowed a water hose and, below the porthole, a helmet in a rack. The pipe with the curved top to the right of the helmet is a fuel-oil tank vent; other such vents are at intervals along the bulkhead.

The depth charge on the K-gun is chained to an arbor: a curved tray with a shaft that is inserted into the barrel of the projector. When the impulse charge is fired, the expanding gases enter the barrel and propel the arbor and depth charge away from the ship.

A K-gun loaded with a Mk. 9 depth charge, a ready rack full of more Mk. 9 depth charges, and a loading davit are viewed from above. Impulse charges with three different weights of powder were used to propel the depth charges to varying ranges from the ship: approximately 60, 90, and 150 yards. The dome-shaped cap on the base of the projector was removed to load the impulse charge and access the firing controls. The K-guns also could be fired from the bridge. Once the Mk. 9 depth charge was fired, the arbor fell away from it, allowing the depth charge to sink unimpeded to the desired depth for detonation.

USS *Kidd* Specifications	
Laid down	October 19, 1942
Launched	February 28, 1943
Commissioned	April 23, 1943
Decommissioned	December 10, 1946, San Diego
Recommissioned	March 28, 1951, San Diego
Decommissioned	June 19, 1964, Philadelphia
Stricken from Navy list	December 1974
Arrived Baton Rouge	May 23, 1982
Opened as memorial	August 27, 1983
Displacement	2,050 tons standard (1943), 2,940 tons full load (1943)
Length	376 feet, 5 inches, overall
Beam	39 feet, 7 inches, maximum
Draft	13 feet, 9 inches, design; 17 feet, 9 inches, maximum
Boilers	4× Babcock and Wilcox three-drum express type
Turbines	2× General Electric geared turbines
Propellers	2× three-blade, 12 feet, 3 inches in diameter
Armament as built	Guns: 5× 5-inch/38-caliber, 3× 40 mm twin, 10× 20 mm single, plus 2× 21-inch quintuple torpedo launchers
Armament in August 1945	Guns: 5× 5-inch/38-caliber, 3× 40 mm twin, 2× 40 mm quad, 7× 20 mm dual, plus one 21-inch quintuple torpedo launcher
Wartime crew	330 officers and men

These octagonal-shaped objects stored on the ready rack for depth charges are arbors, showing the part of the tray upon which the mine is secured prior to firing. The arbors were expendable, each one sinking to the bottom of the ocean once fired.

The port side of the aft deckhouse is viewed from the main deck, facing forward. In the left background are K-guns and depth-charge ready racks. At the center is a float-net basket, above which is the aft twin 40 mm mount and, at top left, 5-inch mount number 4.

This door at the port aft corner of the aft deckhouse leads into a fan room and passageway into the next compartment forward, the ammunition-handling room for 5-inch/38-caliber gun mount number 4, which is located directly above that room.

The number 4 5-inch/38-caliber gun mount is viewed from the port side of the main deck, facing forward. This is the aft 5-inch mount on the aft deckhouse. To the left are the upper level of the aft deckhouse, the aft twin 40 mm gun platform, and the mainmast.

This is the aft 5-inch/38-caliber gun mount, number 5, on USS *Kidd.* It is mounted on the main deck, aft of the aft deckhouse, and, since it was susceptible to overfiring from 5-inch mount 4 in the background, it had a blast hood over the mount captain's hatch.

The front of 5-inch/38-caliber gun mount number 5 is viewed. The oval doors at the upper corners of the top plate of the gun shield protect the openings for the pointer's (*right side, as seen here*) and trainer's (*left side*) sights. Below those doors are windows for the pointer and trainer, equipped with protective doors, shown open here. On each side of the bottom plate of the front of the shield is a hinged access door, to permit crewmen to repair or perform maintenance on mechanisms in the lower front of the gun mount.

The stern of *Kidd* is observed from the starboard side. The key features on deck are depth-charge racks, loading davits, twin 20 mm gun mounts within a splinter shield, and the flag staff, from which the US flag was usually flown when the ship was in port. Projecting from the side of the hull is a propeller guard made from channel iron, with braces. There was a propeller guard on each side of the hull, and they acted like simple bumpers to prevent damage to the propellers when the ship was maneuvering close to a docking facility or another ship.

In another photo of the stern taken from a slightly different angle, it is noticeable how the aft end of the splinter shield for the aft 20 mm guns tapers in toward the longitudinal centerline of the ship. This splinter shield has a heart shape when viewed from above.

The aft twin 20 mm gun mounts and the splinter shield that encloses them are viewed facing aft. Two ready-service 20 mm ammunition boxes are within the splinter shield. To the right is a hatch with a davit for lowering heavy objects. A ventilator is at the center.

The splinter shield and the starboard aft twin 20 mm gun mount are viewed close-up. An M2 talker's helmet is in the rack on the outside of the splinter shield. A scupper is at the bottom of the splinter shield to the left to allow water on the deck to flow out.

The splinter shield and aft twin 20 mm gun mounts on the fantail are observed from the port side. All the 20 mm gun mounts on USS *Kidd* are Mk. 24 Mod. 5 tripod-type mounts. Originally, all of the ship's 20 mm guns were on pedestal-type mounts.

The aft port 20 mm gun mount is viewed from the centerline of the deck, with the hatch davit to the right. These guns use the tripod mounts with fixed trunnion heights. This mount has a ring sight. To the left is a 20 mm ready-service ammunition box.

The same twin 20 mm gun in the preceding photo is viewed from the gunner's perspective. The shoulder rests have padding and are fitted with the straps that would secure the gunner to the piece. A good view is offered of the rears of the magazines.

Three ready-service ammunition boxes for the aft twin 20 mm gun mounts are mounted on the fantail; two are within the splinter shield, and the other is just outside it. These boxes are the protected type, with additional protective plates on the sides of the boxes.

The port aft twin 20 mm gun mount is viewed from its rear right quarter, giving a close view of the two steel plates that compose the shield of the mount. The coil-type recoil springs are visible within the barrel sleeves of the guns.

On the fantail are two release tracks, also called roll-off racks, for depth charges and, inboard of them, two depth-charge ready racks. The release tracks relied on their sloping angles and gravity to allow depth charges to roll off into the ocean. The davit with block and tackle by each depth-charge rack was used for loading the heavy depth charges.

Viewed from the center of the fantail are the port depth-charge ready rack and, beyond it, the port release track. In the release track and resting on the deck in the foreground are Mk. 9 depth charges. The drum-shaped Mk. 6 depth charge also could be accommodated.

The starboard depth-charge release track is viewed facing aft; the starboard ready rack is to the right. The release track assembly has two lower tracks and two upper guide rails. Detents at the rear of the lower pair of tracks released the depth charges.

The port depth-charge ready rack and release tracks are viewed closer-up. The release of depth charges from the fantail stations could be accomplished manually at the release tracks or remotely from the bridge. To the left of center is a ventilator.

The starboard release track and ready rack are viewed looking from the centerline of the fantail toward the side. On the guide rails at the top of the release track are pawls, which kept the depth charges in the track from rolling forward in rough seas.

In this close-up view of the port depth-charge release track, the pawl assemblies are clearly visible, spanning the guide rails on top. Mounted to the deck to the lower center of the photo is the track-control unit, by which the depth charges were manually released.

Mk. 9 depth charges are stored on the fantail. The rings around the tail fins reinforced the fins, and the outer tail ring as well as the nose-support ring provided the mechanical means for these teardrop-shaped depth charges to roll down a release track.

At the stern is the flag staff, from which the ensign would fly between 0800 hours and sunset when the ship was at anchor. When the ship was underway, the ensign was flown from the battle flag staff on the rear of the aft smokestack. Next to the flag staff on a short pole is the anchor light. One of several anchor lights on board, this was a white light, visible all around, that was illuminated when the ship was at anchor. To the rear of the anchor light pole is the stern light, in a housing that allowed it to be viewed from a specific sector to the rear.

Viewed from the starboard side, the pilothouse was the navigational control center of the ship, where the ship was steered and orders were sent to the engine room specifying the engine order and speed. During wartime, usually nine men occupied the pilothouse.

In the port forward corner of the pilothouse is a chart table with a flexible light over it. To the center is the radar repeater, with an M1 helmet covering the screen of the radar scope on top of it. The radar repeater presented a view of air- and surface-search results.

The ship's steering wheel, manned by the helmsman, is to the left, with a gyrocompass repeater and binnacle in front of it. On the stand to the right is the engine-order telegraph, by which signals were sent to the engine room concerning engine order and speed.

These are electrical switch panels on the starboard side of the rear bulkhead in the pilothouse. The switch panel for the ship's navigational lights is to the left. Two intercom boxes are at the center. More electrical control boxes are to the right.

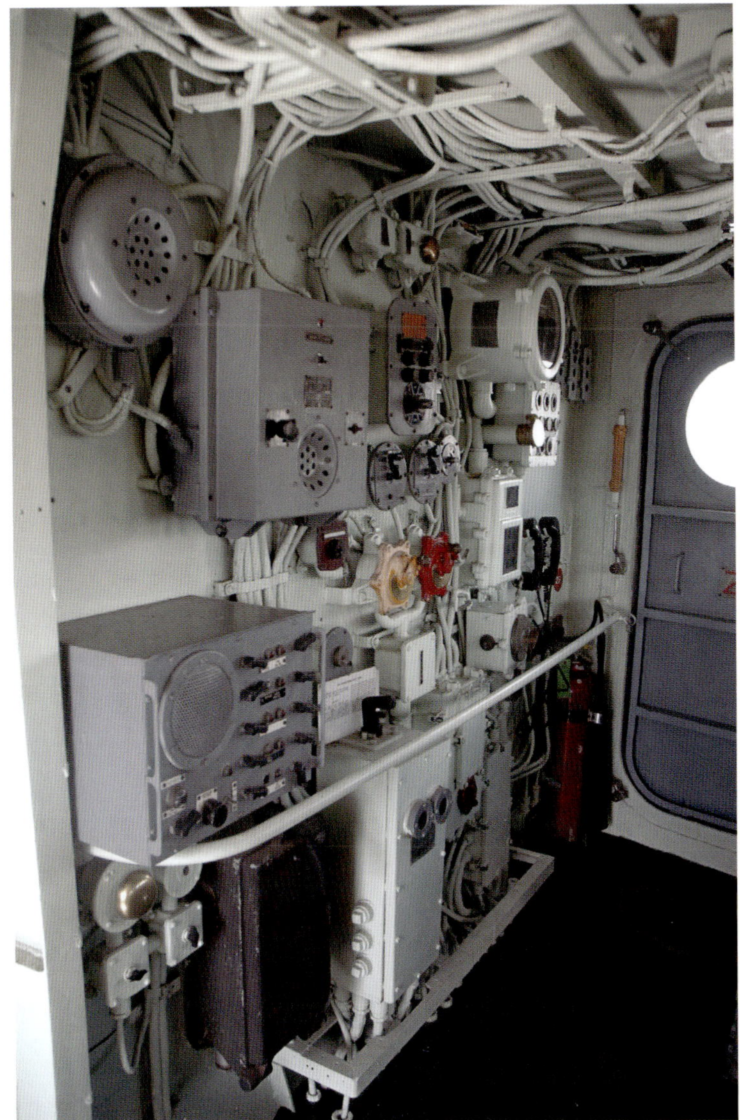

This is the port half of the aft bulkhead in the pilothouse. It is largely covered with communications and electrical controls and panels. Alarm bells, a voice tube for sending vocal signals to other parts of the ship, and two telephone handsets are also on the bulkhead. Routed along the ceiling frames are a maze of electrical lines. To the right is a door leading out onto the bridge.

Aft of the pilothouse and in the same deckhouse is the captain's sea cabin. When the ship was at sea, this was where the captain was berthed. These quarters were cramped and spartan, with a bunk, shelves, and lighting. Radio equipment is mounted in the corner.

The sonar control room is aft of the captain's sea cabin. *Kidd* had a sonar unit toward the bottom of the hull, which sent out sound waves that would "ping" off enemy submarines, enabling the sonar operators to detect their locations.

Radio Central was *Kidd's* main radio-receiving and radio-transmitting center. Here, operators would listen for coded messages and type transcripts of them for decoding. Operators had to be extremely vigilant to record all messages the ship received.

In addition to the obvious suite of transmitters and receivers, Radio Central also houses teletype equipment. The crescendo of radio gear, typewriters, and teletypes operating simultaneously is but one of the reasons radio operators were furnished with headsets.

The chart room, adjacent to Radio Central, was the station of the ship's navigators—the quartermasters. The drawers contained a sizable collection of navigational charts of most of the world's oceans. Navigational instruments are on the chart table.

The ship's officers ate their meals in the wardroom, on the main-deck level of the forward superstructure. Unlike enlisted men, they had to pay for their board. The wardroom also served as the main battle-dressing station and emergency surgery room.

The captain's stateroom was the captain's quarters when the ship was in port. Originally, this stateroom was where the combat information center (CIC) is now; when the CIC was installed, the captain's stateroom took over the space occupied by the doctor's stateroom.

With the advent of more-sophisticated electronic sensing equipment during World War II, the US Navy fitted its warships with combat information centers to process this vast new flow of information. The CIC is adjacent to the captain's stateroom.

Located on the main deck aft of the forward smokestack, the galley prepared three meals a day for USS *Kidd's* approximately 330 enlisted men. A stainless-steel sink and counter are in the foreground; to the left is one of three steam kettles in the galley.

Operators in the CIC monitored information on local enemy threats derived from radar, sonar, radio, and visual sightings, and plotted them on a Plexiglas situation board (*right*), giving decision makers in the CIC a real-time visual picture of the tactical situation.

Stoves and bake ovens are arranged against the forward bulkhead of the galley. The floor is painted red because the galley served as a first-aid station during battle; red floors camouflaged blood and could prevent a wounded sailor from going into shock.

Aft of the galley is the laundry, where the enlisted men's and officers' clothing was washed, dried, and pressed. To the left is an extractor, where wet clothes were transferred from the washing machine, to spin out the water and detergent suds from them.

Several crew's quarters were on the first and second platforms. The accommodations were simple, with bunks with thin mattresses and spring frames, and small lockers for clothing and personal gear. In warm climates these quarters were insufferably hot.

The sick bay was a compartment along the midships passage, a transverse corridor on the main deck between the smokestacks. Here, a doctor checked and treated patients during sick call, and a pharmacist prepared prescriptions from a stock of chemicals.

This is the serving area in a crew's mess on the second platform, two levels below the main deck. During World War II, crewmen carried food prepared in the galley down here to be served. During the Korean War, a dumbwaiter was installed to perform this task.

In the ammunition-handling rooms below each 5-inch gun mount, projectiles and powder cartridges were brought up from magazines below and sent up to the guns as needed. The platform at center was where a crewman passed cartridges (*left*) up to the gunhouse.

Inside a 5-inch/38-caliber gun mount, a projectile and a powder cartridge are placed on the loading tray. The power rammer on the top of the right side of the gun housing would ram the ammunition into the breech. To the left is the upper end of the projectile hoist.

The projectile hoist (*center*) and the powder-passer's platform rotated in unison with the gun mount. The projectile hoist was electrohydraulically operated but could be manually operated with the handwheel if the power should fail. A fuse setter was incorporated into the hoist; thus, when the projectiles arrived in the gunhouse, they were ready to be loaded into the guns immediately. The black, radiating shapes on the floor in the preceding photo are nonskid strips, which helped the crewmen avoid slipping while handling ammunition, and served as a warning to stay clear of the rotating hoist and platform. The 5-inch projectiles are stored on the bulkhead.

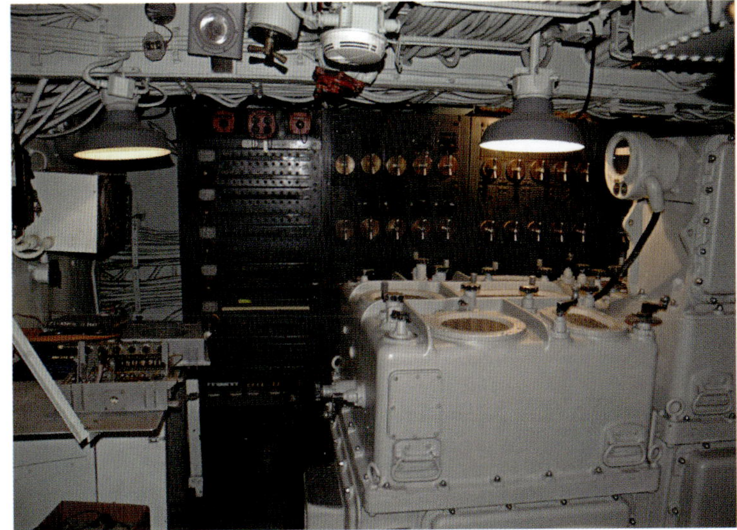

On the first platform is the interior communications plotting room, or IC-PLOT. As the name suggests, this room contained intercom, telephone, and public address equipment, but also the master gyro compass and, *center foreground*, the main-battery computer.

There are two engine rooms on *Kidd*: the forward and the aft. This is the forward engine room, showing a General Electric geared turbine in the center background. The turbines' output is routed through two sets of DeLaval double-reduction gears.

Kidd's steam was provided by four Babcock & Wheeler boilers like this one. Two boilers were located in each fireroom. The boilers were of divided-furnace, single-uptake, three-drum express design. The boilers developed 565 pounds per square inch at 850 degrees Fahrenheit.

Near the stern is the steering compartment, with cylinders that operated the rudder according to signals from the steering wheel in the pilothouse. If the primary steering control were knocked out, the ship could be steered manually from this position.

When the level of the Mississippi River drops during the winter months, the destroyer *Kidd* settles into a specially built cradle, which in effect drydocks the ship for a certain portion of each year. This allows visitors to observe the entire ship, including the part of the hull that is normally submerged. At the time this photo was taken, the ship had only one depth-charge rack at the stern. *Kidd* is a remarkably well-preserved example of the Fletcher class and serves as a tribute to the intrepid destroyer men who served on these "tin cans" in World War II. *USS Kidd collection*